Accelerated Learning

Series Box Set

Three Book Bundle:

Photographic Memory, Accelerated Learning, Speed_Reading

By: Lawrence Franz

Photographic Memory

*How to Improve Memory Skills
and
Remember More of What You Read
and Hear*

By: Lawrence Franz

Table of Contents

Introduction 5

Chapter One: The Human Brain and Memory 12

Chapter Two: Creative Thinking and Visualization

    for Memory 24

Chapter Three: Peg System Memory Techniques 30

Chapter Four: Tips to Remember Names 39

Chapter Five: Mind Mapping Tips 45

Chapter Six: Memory Palace 51

Chapter Seven: General Tips for Improved

    Memory 57

Conclusion 72

Introduction

Memory is a fascinating aspect of human beings and experts are still grappling with the effort of understanding in how many different mindboggling ways our brains work when it comes to storing and recalling data. Scientists are struggling to comprehend how some memories remain fresh long after the data has been assimilated into the brain while other memories are forgotten almost immediately after the event is over.

Photographic memory also referred to as eidetic memory, is the ability of the brain to recall any situation with amazing clarity long after the event is over and done with. It is like there is an image of the information deeply embossed in the mind and which can be recalled at will. The memory (in the form of an image) remains clear and sharp for a long time to come and usually is an effect that happens when some people are exposed to the same circumstance or event repeatedly.

There is no perfect understanding as to why some people can remember better without any training while others struggle to remember information even after some amount of training. However, studies have proven that repeated familiarity with the information significantly improves memory and recalling capabilities for nearly everyone.

Psychologists argue that everyone has some powers of eidetic or photographic memory; only that some of us don't have as much reel to capture and store the information as others. If scientists and experts are struggling so hard to comprehend this rather nebulous concept, then the average man is bound to have even more difficulties in that direction.

However, it is clear that people with an eidetic memory are able to remember a lot of information with a lot more accuracy than someone who does not have eidetic photographic memory. According to some experts, young children use their eidetic memory powers to help them remember things. These experts say these eidetic powers are replaced during the growth phase by verbal strategies such as rehearsing names, lists, and other details mentally.

Whatever the name used, the power of having a great memory cannot be undermined. Some classic examples of how phenomenal memory skills help some people achieve extraordinary success:

- Chess masters can play multiple opponents blindfolded; all the needed information is in their head
- Card sharks can memorize the order of a deck after it is shuffled in a couple of minutes or less

The following famous people are known to have had photographic memories, which helped them catapult to amazing success:

Nikola Tesla – This 19th-century inventor himself said that his photographic memory was one of his quirks that made him successful. He had no problem learning up entire books, and he also experienced brilliant flashes of light with hallucinating effects. Tesla admitted to having detailed visuals of his inventions much before he started tinkering with the raw materials.

Theodore Roosevelt – Known to a speed reader, Theodore Roosevelt could recite any pages of newspapers (not just the articles) as if he was reading from them. His amazing speed reading capabilities allowed him to devour 2-3 books a day.

Kim Peek – The inspiration behind the movie, Rain Man, starring Justin Hoffman, Kim Peek is believed to have memorized every word in every book he ever read (about 9000 in total). He could read each side of an open page with one eye making it possible for him to read at unprecedented speeds.

Psychiatrists who studied and analyzed Kim Peek's abilities said that his actions proved flexibility of the human brain is far, far more than we initially thought. Like many excessively brilliant people, Kim Peek had a disability in one aspect of the brain, which seems to have been compensated with remarkable capabilities in another part.

Jerry Lucas – A top basketball player of his times (from 1962 to 1974), Lucas' other skill is his remarkable memory. He has written numerous books on memory building techniques and helped many people tips on how to make intangible and abstract information into animations and pictures with which you can make learning easy, fun, and deeply ingrained in your mind.

The good thing about memory is that you can improve it through the practice of tricks, tips, and memorization techniques, which is what this book is all about. Having a good memory helps us improve our productivity and efficiency. Just sit back, relax, and imagine a world where your memory is clear and sharp.

- You will not have to face the frustration and embarrassment of meeting someone and not being able to recall either the person's face or her name even as she exuberantly hugs you and addresses you by name as if you were her best friend
- 'I forgot' will never be an excuse in your life.
- Your best friend's or your partner's birthday card has reached him/her right on time keeping your relationship smooth and happy.
- You will know exactly where you put your glasses or your car keys and you will not waste time and energy trying to remember these mundane but important details.
- You will not have to walk into a room and wonder why you went there at all because your mind has chosen to forget the reason, thanks to your below-average recalling capabilities.
- All your passwords, PIN numbers, and other confidential data are stored safely in your head ready to be commanded at your beck and call.

Proven Benefits of Memorization Techniques

This book is full of memorization tips and tricks. How exactly do these techniques improve your memory powers? Here are some of the things that memorization techniques do for you and your brain:

They train your brain to remember – There is a memory technique that calls for you to memorize poetry. Although this exercise might seem like a waste of effort, it is an essential task that drives and trains your mind to remember things. These memory techniques exercise your brain by empowering it to retain more data than before.

They challenge your brain – Working out at the gym challenges your physical body. Memorizing techniques are the workout for your brain challenging its limits and compelling it to achieve higher levels of mental fitness. Memory techniques act as mental gymnastics exercises in improving your brain's agility and alertness.

Learning by heart improves neural plasticity – Researchers have proved that rote learning for extended periods of time helps to improve recall capacity. Repeated rote learning activates the hippocampus in the brain and improves neural plasticity enhancing the cognitive function of your brain.

Storing information for easy recall frees up your thinking power – Students who can easily recall functions, equations and definitions will be able to free up their brain power to focus on problem-solving and application-based questions. When the foundational aspects of knowledge are firmly established in the brain, you can move on to bigger and better things.

So, whether you are a student, teacher, lawyer, translator, accountant or are in any other profession, use the memory tips and techniques mentioned in this book and take your productivity and efficiency to the next level.

Chapter One:
The Human Brain and Memory

What happens in our brain when we make memories or when we try to recall them? Some people think our brain works like a computer and liken the recalling aspect to jamming a flash drive into some kind of a slot near the vicinity of your face. However, it is not that simple or convenient to understand the concept of memory storage and recall in the human brain.

You could compare your brain with Santa's sack filled with toys to be delivered at different places to different people. But, in reality, our memory is not one solid element that is stored in one place. Memory is a collection of images, conversations and ideas that are distinct from each other and need different kinds of tools for storage and recall. Moreover, the brain combines these memories in an amazingly varied number of ways to help you recover the information when you need it.

Short-Term Memory

Commonly, we think of short-term memory as being our ability to store and recall information within a short duration; typically, from a few hours to a day. However, short-term memory is, technically speaking, more fleeting than that. Short-term memory, as per scientific definition, is said to last between 15-30 seconds; akin to writing your name with a sparkler in the air. Once, the effect of the sparkler is gone, the thought is gone. Anything beyond this time is considered to be long-term memory.

If we were to use computer language, short-term memory is like the RAM – Random Access Memory that holds the data that is currently used for immediate actions and thoughts. These short-term memories can be in the form of information our senses are sending to our brain or recalling of some events or ideas that are needed for the current task you are engaged in.

Neuroscience theorizes that these short-term memory activities are performed by the neural interactions happening in the prefrontal cortex situated in front of the brain. Other aspects of short-term memory include:

- ***Limited capacity or space*** – Based on multiple observational studies, experts argue that short-term memory can hold not more than seven elements in its storage space

- ***Limited duration*** – The memory at this level is very fleeting and can easily and quickly be lost by distraction or with time
- ***Encoding*** - is primarily in the acoustic form, and even visual ideas are changed to sounds

Items in the short-term memory can be extended through repeated acoustic encoding or repeating verbally which is called rehearsing. When repeating the information is stopped, then the item is erased from the short-term memory, which is reflective of its limited duration capability. The active processes that take place in short-term memory include:

- ***Recalling information from long-term memory*** – For example, if you need to fill your father's name in on an application form, the process in your short-term memory will retrieve this data from the long-term memory.
- ***Rehearsing data*** – As discussed above, if you need to keep the information in your short-term memory for a longer duration than its current capability, then you would have to rehearse it through verbal encoding
- ***Selective attention to sensory memory*** – For example, if you are sitting on a chair, you will not remember the pressure of the sitting position on your bottom unless you focus your attention on the sense.

Moreover, as scientific research developed on human memory, the concept of short-term memory has taken on a new name and additional aspects. It is referred to as working memory and includes the following aspects too:

- The fact that short-term memory has different processes could mean that there are different areas for these functions
- People with damaged brains lose memory selectively while some other elements function normally suggesting that memory span, rehearsing, re-coding and transferring data to long-term memory use different parts of the brain system, and these are independent of each other
- Although at the basic level, short-term memory does not seem to be connected to reading, reasoning, verbal processing or other such types of complex intelligence elements, studies have shown that, at a more complex level, these aspects of memory and intelligence take place at the short-term memory span too

Long-Term Memory

In this place, the memory becomes a 'physical thing.' If short-term memory can be likened to your computer's RAM, then long-term memory can be likened to its hard-drive where everything in your life is stored. Long-term memory has a physical presence in the brain and is not only dependent on any kind of specific neural activity.

In long-term memory, neurons connect with each other physically through synapses that endure whether they are used or not. Remember, in the short-term memory, if the data is not used, it is out of that space? Long-term memory is the opposite; even if you don't use the data, it remains in that space. Long-term memory can be further split into two types; implicit memory and explicit memory

Implicit Memory – deals with skills and habits that are done automatically and without thought. Examples of activities handled by implicit memory include driving a car, rolling a cigarette, swinging a bat, typing on the keyboard, humming an old and familiar tune, or any kind of habits that you have developed. This kind of memory is unconscious and unintentional.

Recalling from implicit memory happens without your conscious knowledge. You don't have to stop and think how to roll a cigarette or swing a bat. Riding a bicycle is a classic example of implicit memory. If you have to ride a bike for the first time after a long gap, then too, you will be able to hop on to a cycle and ride effortlessly.

Explicit Memory – deals with ideas that you intentionally try to remember and are conscious of the efforts that go into making memories and recalling them. For example, trying to remember a scientific formula for your exam is an example of using your explicit memory. We use our explicit memory every day; from trying to recall the time of the doctor's appointment or studying for a test, etc. Also referred to as declarative memory, this kind of memory requires you conscious and explicit efforts to remember and recall.

Examples of explicit memory include learning for a test or trying to remember what was taught in your physics class, recalling the phone number of your friend or that incident in high school that happened a few years ago or the capital of France or the current US President, etc. Explicit memory can be further divided into two types; episodic memory and semantic memory.

Episodic memory involves episodes and events that happened to you such as what happened during your high school or college or in your love life. *Semantic memory* involves general data and information such as the capital of France or the name of the US President.

An illustration to discern between episodic and semantic memory is as follows: recalling the fact that Paris is the capital of France is a semantic memory; recalling how you fell ill on your Paris trip last year is an episodic memory.

Encoding and Consolidation

Encoding is a complex process that weaves through millions of neurons and neural activity that help in memorizing things in such a way that you can recall them later on. When we actually make an effort to remember something, then it's the long-term memory that we concerned about. So, how do long-term memories form? The first step in creating long-term memories is to encode the information quickly failing which it will be lost just like breath on a mirror or the writing of your name in the air with a sparkler.

Several parts of the brain play a part in the process of encoding and consolidating information. The most important parts of the brain involved in this process are the hippocampus, the amygdala, and the cerebellum. Let us look at each of them in a bit of detail for better understanding:

The hippocampus – is that region of the brain that is responsible for forming new memories. It is also that place in the brain in which new neurons are generated regularly. The hippocampus connects and bonds all the new events and data and forms synaptic connections and encodes them into a new memory. A good analogy is someone knitting a rich and complex tapestry in real-time.

However, the hippocampus does not treat all information equally. The things that are 'important' get preference over things that are not so critical. For example, the hippocampus will prioritize those memories that have a strong emotional bond (maybe the date and amount of your salary) for you than something more routine or incomprehensible such as your daily commute to office or the lyrics of a foreign language song.

The hippocampus is very selective in its approach to encoding new memories because it is always very busy, and prioritizing is the only way it can function effectively. After the information is encoded and consolidated, it ceases to be in the hippocampus. Studies have revealed that the hippocampus does not play a crucial role in memory retention after the consolidation process.

Any damage to the hippocampus results in difficulties in the realm of making new memories. However, some studies revealed that these people can recall older memories because as new memories are formed, the neuron synapses that represent older memories seem to get pushed further into the cortex.

The amygdala – is known to be involved in memory consolidation, or more specifically, modulation, which is the intensity with which the memory is stored in the brain. Specifically, it is noted that the arousal of emotion after a particular incident enhances the depth of consolidation of the memory. The greater the emotional arousal, the stronger the memory consolidation. However, even if the amygdala is damaged, encoded memories can be recalled.

The cerebellum – is known to be responsible for learning structured and procedural memory such as routine and practiced skills and motor skills such as playing a musical instrument, riding a cycle, or driving a car. Damage to the cerebellum can result in the loss of motor and coordination control.

So, a person with damage in his hippocampus might be able to recall how to play the piano will not be able to recall other facts of his life. And, a person with a damaged cerebellum might be able to recall old facts from his life but may have forgotten to play the piano, as earlier.

Similar kinds of memories tend to clump together; visual memories close to the visual cortex, spoken memories close to the language centers, etc. Moreover, there is an accumulation of redundancy where you could have the same memory stored in different ways. Each time you activate these memories, they get stronger than before. Memories are not stored like books in a library; they are continuously tweaked and updated.

Memory and Emotions

The various memory-based studies have found one very intriguing aspect that influences our brain's ability to remember and recall information; our emotional state at the time our brain received this information. Emotions are also known to help in retrieving the data when we revisit it. Putting ourselves in the same frame of mind as it was when the event happened is believed to make recalling easy.

Studies have proven that emotionally charged memories last longer and are easier to recall than those memories, which have no emotional, connect. When we feel anger, happiness, or delight, then we have a more vivid recollections of what happened than the routine everyday tasks that have little or no emotional connection for us.

For example, you can recall the events of your first date that happened many years ago more vividly than the scene of filling your cat's dinner bowl with food just yesterday or how many beers you had last Saturday or what color socks you wore to the office yesterday. Our brains can retain and retrieve those memories that are emotionally charged. In addition to emotions, other aspects that affect our memory include moods and attention.

Recalling Memories from the Recesses of the Brain

So, how can we recall specific bits of information from the big chunk of data that is scattered all over the brain? It might look like the so-called old memories have turned to dust because you have forgotten a lot of things such as old passwords, addresses, deadlines, etc. What you must remember is that you haven't forgotten them; your recalling ability has simply become reduced in intensity. It's like a glove that you have forgotten where you put. You still own the glove; you simply don't know where you have put it.

Recalling memories is a mysterious brain function, and how information from the dark recesses of our brain is accessed is a work-in-progress project for neuroscientists. It is uncertain how our frontal cortex of the brain accesses the stored information and makes it relevant for use in the present. However, it is quite certain that the more you use this capability, the easier it is to find the data.

Therefore, it makes sense to work on and perfect a few memory improvement techniques to keep our brains active, and also to leverage the benefits of a more productive and meaningful life.

Chapter Two: Creative Thinking and Visualization for Memory

How does creative thinking and visualization help in improving your memory? Many studies have revealed that visualization and creative thinking are directly connected to memory. When we try to remember things from our past, we access our episodic memory, which, in turn, helps in triggering creative, divergent thinking.

Episodic memory helps us to time travel mentally into the past as well as the future thereby building our creativity while improving our memory. Essentially, when we delve deep into detailed aspects of our past or into the dreams for our future, our brain is primed to think creatively.

In the same way, our brain is able to remember better through visualization and creative thinking techniques because humans can remember images better than written or verbal information. For example, if you have shifted homes, you will notice that you can clearly remember the design and details of the living room and bedrooms in each house. However, you may not be able to recall street names, door numbers, or telephone numbers with the same vividness.

Images are concrete and tangible whereas raw information in the form of written or spoken words is quite abstract making it more difficult to store and recall the latter format. However, it is possible to convert these abstract elements into tangible forms through memory techniques based on visualization and creative thinking.

These images become your mental hooks using which you can retrieve information from your long-term memory archives. While one of the primary reasons visualization techniques for memory work is that our brain remembers images well, there are other reasons too. Visualization techniques help to improve other aspects of memory including repetition and concentration.

So, if you have problems with concentration, visualization techniques are great remedies to get better at it. When you use visualization methods to remember some things, you are compelled to keep your focus on that process; effectually, you have no choice but to focus on your task. Creating mental images is a powerful focusing exercise. Additionally, as you keep exposing your mind repeatedly on the item for which you are creating visual images, the repetitive aspect of memorization is exercised.

Repetition is a key element for memorization. For example, if you meet someone for the first time, and she mentions her name only once, you are quite likely to forget the name. However, during the conversation, if the individual repeats her name more than once, it is quite likely you will not forget it. However, people don't really help us out like this, do they?

Creating mental images makes you repeat each detail of the memory you are making, again and again, to ensure each image is crystal clear and easily recallable when you need it. Therefore, creative thinking and visualization techniques help you increase your memory powers because of the following reasons:

- The human brain finds it easier to remember concrete, tangible images rather than intangible, vague written or spoken words
- Creating images improves your focusing capability; an important aspect of memory skills
- Continuous review of the images will help to reinforce the original memory repeatedly thereby improving memory skills

Moreover, visualization techniques are not difficult to turn into habit. Initially, it might take some time to create images for everything. However, as you practice each day, you will find it increasingly easy to associate memories with images. You will be able to do it almost unconsciously with sufficient practice.

Remembering Types of Volcanoes

Here are some examples of connecting images with complex names. Suppose you need to remember the shape of each type of volcano.

There are three types of volcanoes including cinder cones, shield volcanoes, and stratovolcanoes. Now, your job is to remember the shape of stratovolcanoes so that you can recall it whenever when you need to. Cinder cones form quickly and are small structures consisting of ash and cinders. Shield volcanoes are flat and wide, like a shield, and stratovolcanoes are very high with a pointed peak.

- Cinder volcanoes – cinder and small
- Shield volcanoes – flat and wide (like a shield)
- Stratovolcanoes – high and pointed (like a hill)

Examples of stratovolcanoes include Mount Fiji and Mount Ranier. Now, how can you remember strato and connect it to the 'high and pointed?' Well, here is a tip. Strato sounds like 'straight-O,' and you can imagine a line of O's marching up the pointed-peaked tall high in a straight line.

This image you have created will help you connect stratovolcanoes with 'high and pointed' helping you recognize the picture anywhere you see it. The clearer the image of the memory in your head, the easier it will be to recall. Moreover, the sillier, larger, and more imaginative the picture is, the easier to remember and recall.

More pictures and word-connections

Here are some wild ways of creating images with simple words that illustrate the wild aspect of visualization techniques and improved memory. You can use similar techniques to remember big and complex words:

Charts – Divide this word as char + 'tz' (sounds similar). Char means something burned and black, and 'tz' sounds like the letter zee. So, to remember the word 'charts' you could visualize a huge Z which is completely black and charred.

Source – Source sounds like sour + sea; so how about a lemon-filled ocean?

Data – Data pronounced loosely sounds like 'day' + 'tie.' So, an image of the sun (it is out during the day) trying hard to wear a tie can help you remember the word day + tie which, in turn, because of the association in your mind, you will be able to recall the word, 'data.'

So, like this, you must try and connect complex words with images, which will create a mental hook connecting the word, and the image in your mind making it easy to remember and recall. It might appear bizarre initially for the novice. It is this 'wild' perception that actually creates the right hooking system for excellent recall later on.

Moreover, these visualization techniques are used by performers to achieve superhuman capabilities. If you can achieve even a fraction of that success, your productivity levels will improve significantly.

Chapter Three:
Peg System Memory Techniques

The peg system helps you to remember lists of things like school work, to-do-lists, and other order-based tasks very easily. The peg system also creates an ordered filing format in your brain making it easier to retrieve the required data when needed.

The peg system connects new information by associating it with old data that is already deeply embedded in your mind. Such old data which is used for pegging new data could be the alphabets from A to Z or numbers from 1 to 20, etc. A peg is like a mental hook where you hang the information onto the old information so that you can access it easily.

For example, look at the numbers 1 to 10. If you associate an important memory item with number five, then all you need to do is remember number 5, and your brain will recall the associated item. Before we go into peg system techniques, here are some important elements:

It helps you remember the new data – Unlike rote learning where you simply mug up the data and hope to remember the order correctly, the peg system will connect what you know very well, and help you recall what you need which is the new data. It acts like a loci system by being in the center of all the important things in your life and connecting them to the new data as and when they are added.

It allows you to retrieve information from memory directly – Using the peg system, you can run through the items using the old data, and pick out the one you need directly. You simply run through the entire link until you get to the item that is needed immediately. For example, if you are talking about the list of nerves in the cranial system, and you know the fifth one is the trigeminal nerve, then #5 is connected to it, which becomes your peg system.

You can reuse the peg systems repeatedly – An amazing thing about our brain is that it can associate the same peg system to remember a multitude of information. So, you can connect numbers 1-10 to the set of cranial nerves or the geometrical shapes with varying sides, and your brain will connect the number 5 to the trigeminal nerves when you are thinking about biology and will connect it to a pentagon when you are dealing with geometry. Therefore, the same peg system can be used repeatedly to remember many kinds of information.

You can use any kind of peg system for added flexibility – For example, you can use the even numbers (2, 4, 6, 8...) to remember something, and use odd numbers (1, 3, 5, 7...) for others. This way, you can add flexibility, and also have something unique to remember each type of information as well.

How Does the Peg System Work

It is impossible for an average human being to forget numbers and alphabets, right? Peg systems connect new data to these unforgettable lists to help you remember and recall. However, the problem with numbers and alphabets is that they are abstract forms of data; they are not concrete or tangible objects, and therefore difficult to remember if used directly. The peg system allows you to give tangible forms and shapes to this kind of abstract data.

For example, using rhyming peg words, you can connect numbers to tangible objects such as One-sun, two-shoe, three-tree, and more. To recall the list, simply run through the numbers connect the object to the numbers and find what you are looking for. Then, to remember a list by connecting it to the objects you have given to your peg system. Let us look at a few peg systems for illustration purposes:

The Number-Rhyme Peg System

For each of the numbers from 1-10, find the name of an object that you can easily relate to. The following list is a commonly used peg system number:

- One – sun, bun, gun
- Two – Shoe, zoo, glue
- Three – tree, sea, bee
- Four – door, store
- Five – hive, wife, knife
- Six – sticks, pigs, bricks
- Seven – heaven,
- Eight – gate, plate, skate
- Nine – vine, sign, mine, wine
- Ten – hen, pen

Now, suppose you need to remember the following list; egg, motorbike, plate, shirt, book, coconut, mobile phone, ice cream, mirror, and umbrella. Here are some tips to create a peg system for this list:

- You are frying an egg with the sun's rays streaming into the kitchen – the sun is connected to the first item on the list viz. the egg

- The motorbike runs over your pretty shoes squashing them and rendering them useless – the second list item on the list is connected to the shoe
- Plates are hanging from the tree and are banging against each other as the branches are swaying wildly in the wind – the 3rd item, plate, is connected to tree
- You are covering the gap between the door and the floor to prevent buzzing mosquitoes from entering your house – 4th item connected to door
- A huge bloody knife is stuck out of your Math book because you are so angry that you cannot remember the formulae – 5th item and knife
- You are flinging coconuts on the pigs that disturb you with their grunting while you sleep – 6th item coconut connected to pigs
- The angel from heaven is calling you on your mobile phone – 7th item, mobile phone, is linked through the imagery to heaven
- An ice-cream cone is stuck on your gate because you don't want your mother to know you are eating it – 8th item – ice-cream connected to gate
- A madman is using red wine to clean his mirror, and all the reflections in the mirror

are also appearing red – 9th item connected to wine
- A big fat hen is running around in the farm with an umbrella stuck in her feathers as it doesn't want to get wet – 10th item connected to hem

Now, can you recall the seventh item? Well, seven, heaven, angel calling your mobile phone; therefore the seventh item is mobile phone! Try this exercise randomly, and you will notice you are getting better with each attempt. Tips for numbers 11-20:

- Eleven – Leaven,
- Twelve – Elf, Shelf
- Thirteen – thirsting, hurting
- Fourteen – courting, fording
- Fifteen – lifting, fitting
- Sixteen – licking, Sistine
- Seventeen – deafening, leavening
- Eighteen – waiting, aiding
- Nineteen – pining, knighting
- Twenty – Plenty, penny (to rhyme with the slang way of saying twenny)

The Number-Shape Peg System

This is similar to the number-rhyme peg system except that you use the shape of the number to connect. For numbers 1-10, the connections will be something like this:

- 1 – shape of a stick
- 2 – shape of a duck or swan floating in water
- 3 – The top part of the heart-shape
- 4 – shape of a boat with its sails unfurled
- 5 – the shape of a hook
- 6 – shape of a golf stick
- 7 – the shape of the edge of a cliff
- 8 – shape of an hourglass
- 9 – shape of a balloon at the end of a stick
- 10 – figure of a fork and a plate kept next to each other

Now, suppose you have to remember a list in which the second item is a tomato. So, here is what you can imagine; a tomato dancing on the back of a beautiful white swan on a clear blue lake. So, the connection here is the swan, which is the shape of #2. You can form your own visuals using the techniques given in the Number-Rhyme peg system (of the tomato example) for the rest of the names in the list you need to remember.

Alphabet Peg System

You already know the alphabets and so can recall them with ease, and therefore, they can be used as an excellent memory pegging system. Typically, there are two ways you can use the alphabet peg system; one is using the concrete meaning of the word you associate the alphabet with, and two, based on sound-alike words.

Here are the alphabets followed by 1) the concrete meaning associated with the alphabet, and 2) the rhyming or similar-sounding word:

- A – Alligator, Hay
- B – Boy, Bee
- C – Cat, See
- D – Dog, Dead
- E – Egg, Eve
- F – Fig, Effort
- G – Goat, Jeep
- H – Hat, Age
- I – Ice, Eye
- J – Jack, Jay
- K – Kite, Key
- L – Log, Ell
- M – Man, Hem
- N – Nut, Hen
- O – Owl, Hoe
- P – Pig, Pea
- Q – Quill, Cue
- R – Rock, Oar
- S – Sock, Sass
- T – Toy, Tea
- U – Umbrella, Ewe
- V – Vane, Veal
- W – Wig, Double you
- X - X-Ray, Axe
- Y – Yak, Wire
- Z – Zoo, Zebra

So, to memorize a list of 26 items using the sound-alike alphabet system, you can imagine the first item to be in the midst, the second one being stung by a bee, and so forth. You can use similar imaging techniques to peg your lists to the items connected to the concrete objects linked to each alphabet.

Like all memory techniques, the peg system is also a skill that gets better with practice and sustained effort. Additionally, if you notice the illustrative examples given to use the peg system, there are plenty of visuals and creative thinking that went into making up the images. So, by combining your visualization techniques and the peg system, you can learn to remember anything you want to remember with ease.

Chapter Four:
Tips to Remember Names

People relationships are a key element to personal and professional success. Whether you are a student, student, teacher, lawyer, translator, accountant, or the CEO of an organization, knowing and recalling people's names can improve the success in your particular field. When you remember someone's name, it tells the person that he or she is important to you, and there is a sense of obligation created to reciprocate this feeling. So, here are some great tips to remember people's names.

Know Your Motivation for Remembering the Concerned Individual's Name

Motivation drives memory. If you don't understand and appreciate the importance of your need to remember a person's name, you will forget it. Imagine this person is carrying a bag with $100,000 in it for your cause. Will you forget this person's name? Of course, you will not. You will delve deep into the recesses of your brain, and use every memory technique to recall his name. Reason for remembering reaps results.

Focus on the Conversation

You will not remember the person you spoke to if you are daydreaming or are distracted during the conversation. Make sure you focus on the conversation and actively participate in it. The primary reason for not remembering people's names is you are not listening. And this is not an issue of memory but mere lack of focus.

The details of any task will not embed in your memory if you are not paying attention. The same holds good for conversations too. Pay attention so that the details of what transpired between the two (including the person's name) get registered in the brain.

Focusing on the conversation includes not being distracted by your internal thoughts. You might be quiet on the outside. But, on the inside (in your mind), a lot of thoughts are going on. Especially, in a panic situation, you end up so worried that you will never remember the person's name at the right time that you could miss out the place where his or her name was mentioned. Focus your entire body and mind on the conversations and don't let thoughts wander off somewhere.

Repeat the Person's Name

Repetition is a powerful memory tool and can be easily used during conversations to remember people's name. For example, if you are introduced to someone called, you can always shake his hand and say, "Pleased to meet you, John," or "Nice to meet you, John." That's the only undeniable opportunity you will get to repeat a person's name.

However, for this tip to be successful, you must focus and pay attention when the person's name was mentioned to you. Conversely, if you get into the habit of repeating people's names during the conversation, you will be forced to focus. So, this tip will help you with both tips.

Another way to repeat the person's name is to use his or her name is to find other opportunities to say it, definitely when you are saying goodbye. Practice makes perfect. You can recollect how this newly met person reminds you of another person who is already in your social circle.

See If You Can Find Something Unique in the Person's Face

Look out for a distinctive feature about the person's face. Perhaps, an unusual nose, the color of his or her eyes, a different hairstyle, large ears, or anything else that seems to stand out for you. Typically, the most outstanding feature you notice the first time you meet someone is the one that you can remember easily later on. Connecting the person's name to the visual feature is a creative visualization technique that you already know to be an effective memory tactic.

Connect the Person's Name with Something You Already Know

Even for a common name like John, you can have something that is important to you to which you can connect and recall easily. For example, if you are an avid Bible reader, you can connect John to John the Baptist or the Gospel of John. If you are an avid follower of politics, you can connect your John to John F. Kennedy. If you love music, link John to John Lennon, and so forth. This connection with someone or something that is close to your heart can help you remember names easily.

Use Visualization Techniques

For example, if the person's (who has curly hair) name is Mr. Bender, imagine him bending over a water tank and getting his curls all wet. If his name is Mr. Baldwin, then imagine a bald man on a winning streak in a poker game. The wilder and crazier the image, the easier it is to remember the person's name. Here are more examples which you can extrapolate as you wish:

- Steve – think of a stove over which he is cooking your favorite dish
- Paul – think of a 'ball' in your favorite game
- Hamilton – think of a ton of ham balancing precariously on his nose
- Dave – connect it to your daily shave
- Margaret – imagine margarine melting down her blonde hair

Make a List of the Names of New People You Met During the Day

At the end of the day, make a note of the names of the people you met on that day, either mentally or a physical list. It might seem like a wasted effort initially, but these small acts are what drive your brain to remember things. When you make an effort to crystallize your thoughts, your brain will find it easier to store it in a place from where you can retrieve the information when you need it later on.

And finally, even before you go on to read the tips on how to remember names, the first step is to commit to yourself that you are going to walk down this path of remembering names. It has to be a commitment from your end to find ways to remember people's names. For example, you cannot use the excuse of a 'bad memory' for not being able to remember and recall names. You have to work at it, and you have to give yourself this commitment.

Moreover, remembering people's name improves people management skills endearing you to the people who are important to you helping you achieve success in your professional and personal relationships.

Chapter Five: Mind Mapping Tips

Mind mapping is a powerful tool to capture your thoughts and give them tangibility. Mind maps are a visual tool that can be used to improve all cognitive functions including learning, analysis, memory and creativity. Mind mapping follows a combination of images, color and visual-spacing aspects to write down and structure information in your brain in such a way that recalling and remembering will become significantly easier.

Instead of simply taking down notes, creating mind maps will help you improve your creativity, remember things clearly, and improve your problem-solving abilities.

What are Mind Maps?

A mind map is a diagrammatic representation of a central idea or theme, which is surrounded by connected information about the central theme. So, for example, if your central idea is poetry, then that takes the center place, and all the connected ideas are placed in a radial structure around it.

The radial branches emerging from the central root idea of poetry are typically the subtopics of the primary topic. So, your subtopics for poetry could include:

- Types of poetry
- Famous poets
- Famous works
- Important publications

Each of these branching out subtopics will have branches of its own. For example, the branch of 'types of poetry' will include sub-branches such as classical poetry, contemporary poetry, etc. Each level of branches get more and more detailed and, finally, they can all be linked together.

Mind maps can be used for a variety of learning, thinking and memory tasks from learning a new subject to planning a career to building better habits, to making your memory more powerful than before. Here are the steps to create a mind map:

Step 1 – Create a Central Concept

The central concept is the beginning point of your mind map, which is the main topic you are going to follow. It should be placed in the middle of your mind map page. An accompanying image of the central topic will enhance the encoding process in your brain making it easier to remember and recall. It is important to take time and effort to personalize your central idea. This customized approach will help in connecting with the other content on the page easier than otherwise.

Step 2 – Now, Build Branches to Your Central Theme

The next logical step to the building of a mind map is to create main branches around your main concept. The main branches are the most important sub-themes associated with the central idea. You can add child branches to each of the main sub-themes to achieve greater depth in your learning.

This ability to keep adding child branches is one of the most attractive aspects of mind mapping. You can keep adding new data over the existing data with each new addition enhancing your knowledge associated with the previous ones. The structure of the mind map will flow as naturally as your thoughts develop. The fluidity that mind mapping offers makes the learning process fun and engaging giving you the flexibility to go as deep as you wish.

Step 3 – Include Keywords

Each time a new branch is added, a new idea should be represented using one word only. The importance of limiting the keyword for each idea is one that cannot be underestimated. With one word to describe an idea, a plethora of associated ideas will flow limitlessly as against using a string of words or a phrase.

For example, if you use the words 'birthday party,' you will be restricted to only those aspects associated with birthday party such as venue, time, date, etc. However, if your idea was represented by only with 'birthday,' then your repertoire of ideas will be more extensive, and you can include cake, invitees, presents, etc.

Moreover, keeping one word per branch will help you chunk all the information regarding that one word under one heading resulting in a more compact mind map. Using keywords also triggers brain connections resulting in improved memory and recall ability.

Step 4 – Color Code Your Branches

Mind mapping involves your entire brain to participate in the learning and memory-retentive process because it combines a broad array of cortical skills ranging from logical to numerical to creativity and more.

When all these cognitive powers overlap and intertwine with each other, your brain functioning becomes more synergetic resulting in optimal output. It is not good to isolate different types of cortical functions as brain development is compromised significantly.

Another way to increase cortical overlap is to color code the branches on your mind map. Color coding helps your brain by connecting the visual skills to the logical, numerical and creative parts helping in the creation of shortcuts. These mental shortcuts in your brain will help you retain the information from the mind map in a clear way and facilitating easy recall.

Additionally, colors enhance the appealing and attractive aspect of your mind map helping you to continuously engage with it as you keep adding more branches as your learning progresses.

Step 5 – Include As Many Images As You Can

By now you know the power of images and your brain's capability to recall images better than the spoken or the written word. Images can convey an entire story and far more information than a whole page of text. Images are processed immediately by our brains and also are visual stimuli for memory recall. Also, images speak a universal language that has the power to cross all linguistic barriers. To leverage these powers of using images, ensure your mind map is covered with as many images as you can put.

Mind maps are excellent memory and learning tools and help you in the following ways:

- They help you remember and recall information of all kinds
- They make you think of all possible connections and drive you to have a brainstorming session with yourself
- They help you stay organized
- They help you see all the connections and links of the primary idea
- They save you time by allowing you to learn using only single words instead of entire sentences
- They fit into only one side of the paper thereby saving you space and keeping all related information in a compact manner
- They help you see the project in its entirety as well as its smaller working parts that seamlessly connect with one another
- They help you add new ideas and thoughts without having to rewrite the entire project

Chapter Six: Memory Palace

Used since the time of the ancient Romans, the Memory Palace is one of the most powerful memory tools that are not only easy to learn but engaging and fun too. It is an extremely useful technique to learn and master to improve your productivity and efficiency irrespective of whether you are a student, lawyer, accountant, or in any other profession.

The principle of the Memory Palace technique is based on the fact that the human brain can easily recollect and remember places that we know. This 'memory palace' is nothing but a favorite location of yours that you recall with ease. This palace can be a room inside your home or your commuting route or any other familiar place that is deeply etched in your mind. The familiarity of the place will act as your guide even as you store information and recall it when needed. Here are some important steps to follow to create your Memory Palace:

Step 1 – Choose Your Memory Palace

The most important thing to bear in mind while choosing your palace is your familiarity with the place. The effectiveness of this technique is entirely dependent on how easy it is for you to wander around your palace and see things clearly in your mind.

Your palace should be a place where you can be present (yes, mentally) at will, anywhere, anytime. The more clearly and vividly you can recall the intricate details of your palace, the more effective this technique will be. An effective first choice is your own home.

You must also create a walking path in your mind palace that is constantly moving around in the way you want it to. The palace should not be a static one; instead, it should be a dynamic one that your mind's eye can travel through with ease.

Therefore, instead of simply focusing on the static outside façade of your home, take a visual trip. For example, watch the emergence of the various places in your home as you walk in through the front door; pass the living room into the corridor that leads into the bedroom even as you catch sight of the dining room to your left. A specific order of the path will also improve the effectiveness of this technique.

Here are some more tips on the kind of memory palace you can choose:

- Possible routes to your workplace.
- Any street in your city that you are familiar with
- Your high school or college – Here you can imagine the various paths leading to your classrooms, the library, the basketball court, and other places that you enjoy being in
- Your office – Imagine the door opening into the main building of your office. Imagine walking down the familiar path to your cabin, saying hi to the different people seated at their desks, and other such scenes
- A park in your neighborhood

Step 2 – Make a List of Distinctive Features

The next step is to pay attention to the various features in your memory palace. For example, if you have chosen your home as your memory palace, then the front door will be the first distinctive feature. Then walk into your house and make a mental note of all the things you can see which could include:

- That picture on the wall
- The dining table

- The open kitchen and its various cabinets

Each of these features will become a memory slot in your palace.

Step 3 – Imprint Your Memory Palace in Your Head

You have to be able to commit to memory all the distinctive features of this memory palace entirely in your mind. There has to be an image deeply imprinted in your head. If visual learning is your strength, then this might not be very difficult for you. For the others, here are a few tips:

- Literally walk through your memory palace (physically, not mentally) and say out loud all the distinctive features along the path
- Next, make a written note of these features, and commit them to memory even as you mentally walk through the memory palace
- Make sure you see the distinctive feature from the same perspective
- When you think your imprint is thorough, repeat it again and again until there is not an iota of doubt

When this imprint of your memory palace is stamped on your mind, you are ready to use it. You can reuse this palace any number of times to remember anything you want to.

Step 4 – Create Associations

Now, that you have deeply entrenched in your mind, create associations for each of the things you need to remember using the tips given in the Peg System (Chapter 3). Each memory peg will be one distinctive feature in your memory palace. Here is an example to illustrate how this works. Suppose we need to make a grocery list with your memory palace. Suppose the list you have in mind is as follows:

- Bacon
- Eggs
- Flour

There are only three items for illustrative purposes. You can use any number of items into your list and remember them with ease. Now, the first three distinctive features in your home memory place are the front door, the picture on the wall, and the dining table. Now, associate the above items as follows:

- Bacon – imagine a huge piece of bacon stuck on your front door and the neighbors are laughing at the scene
- Eggs – Imagine eggs being thrown on that picture on the wall and the gooey insides trickling down the picture

- Floor – Imagine flour being dusted all over your dining table

Now, at the grocer's, when you need to recall these items, walk mentally through your memory palace and recall these vivid associations and the grocery list will come in a flash.

Step 5 – Keep Visiting Your Palace

If you are new to this concept, you might need to have a few rehearsals for the initial memory exercise. Therefore, keep visiting your palace, and keep making mental notes of the distinctive features. As your palace grows, the number of these features will also grow. As you complete one tour of your palace, turn around, and walk in the reverse direction until you reach the starting point of your palace.

The Memory Palace is an effective visual and creative thinking-based memory tool that will never go out of fashion for you because you are dealing with something tangible that you are very familiar with. Moreover, as you keep using your Memory Palace, the familiarity is going to increase enhancing the effectiveness of this memory improvement technique.

Chapter Seven: General Tips for Improved Memory

While visual techniques, mind map techniques, peg systems and memory palaces are specific methods to improve your memory capabilities; there are general health-based and mental exercises that boost your memory. Let us look at some of them in this chapter.

Powerful Memory-Boosting Mental Exercises

Mental activities help your brain to move away from its familiar path of thinking and set up new neural connections thereby improving its functioning and skills. Sticking to the same path of thinking will result in your brain becoming inactive and dull. You have to keep challenging it to new levels and planes of thought.

Memory is like muscle power; if you don't use it, you lose it. Here are many more benefits of indulging in powerful memory-boosting mental exercises:

It teaches you new ways of thinking – Irrespective of how mentally challenging your work is, your brain achieves a sense of familiarity, and cognitive strength will begin to stagnate instead of developing more. The way to break its familiar way of thinking is to make the brain do unfamiliar mental activities, and that is what different kinds of mental exercise will achieve for you.

It challenges your brain – Brain-boosting exercises require you to give your complete attention and focus. For example, playing a musical piece (no matter how hard) that you already know well is not challenging to the brain. However, learning to play a new song (no matter how seemingly easy) challenges your brain to achieve higher levels of thinking and memory skills.

Choose mental activities and games that take you from an easy level slowly to more difficult ones. That way, each time your brain is challenged to do things better than the previous level.

Here are some brain-boosting exercises that you can indulge in as often as you can:

Recalling Self-Tests - Make a list of things you need to do such as a grocery list or to-do list or the names of people in your high school or anything else. Now, arrange them in an order, and use any of the techniques to learn up the list by heart. Now, take a break for an hour, and then try and recall what you have learned. Repeat this exercise as often as you can to improve your memory powers.

Learn to play an instrument or to sing – Music is known to have immense memory-boosting capabilities. Learning music either in the vocal form or playing an instrument is known to improve memory capabilities significantly. Multiple studies connect memory to music. Sometimes, even listening to your favorite music can help in the learning process. However, when you are studying, it is better to listen only to instrumental as lyrics of a song can be quite a distraction.

Do some complex math in your head – Take two 3-digit numbers and try to add them in your head without the help of a calculator or even a paper and pencil. Make it more difficult by indulging in a physical exercise while doing the arithmetic problem. You could choose to increase the intensity of the math problem by multiplying instead of adding.

Learn to cook – Cooking involves the use of multiple sensory organs including touch, smell, sight, and taste. Each of these sensory organs involves the working of different parts of the brain, which is great for optimal brain functioning.

Learn a new language – A new language which involves hearing and talking new words stimulate the brain increasing its functioning and your memory skills.

Indulge in a hobby involving hand-eye coordination – Knitting, painting, assembling a puzzle, drawing, etc. are hobbies that involve hand-eye coordination, which improves brain functioning.

Lifestyle-Related Memory-Boosting Tips
Get Sufficient Sleep

This is the easiest and effective way to boost your memory. After you have learned something new, take a short nap or get a good night's restful sleep. Multiple studies have proven that people who sleep over a new idea or lesson are able to remember much better than those who did not get sleep after the lesson. Sleep is an important phase when the brain is able to not only embed the memories deep within its recesses but also in a way that makes retrieval easy for you.

Sleep resets our brain (much like the save button on your computer applications), and therefore, critical for memory and learning. If you don't enough sleep, the neurons in your brain get overactive with electrical impulses buzzing around crazily making it difficult to register and encode new memories. Sleep is mandatory for the memory consolidation process.

Therefore, late-night cramming before an exam should be avoided as much as possible. Instead, regular study and sufficient sleep work wonders to help you clear exams with flying colors. Researchers also opine that a 45-60 minute nap after learning something new will help in retention and recall by nearly 500%.

Another important aspect of sleep is to know the difference between the amount of sleep you need to get on and the amount you need for optimal functioning of your entire body system including your brain. Here are some important pointers about sleep:

Get a regular sleep schedule – Keep your bedtime and wake-up time constant as much as possible. Avoid breaking your sleep schedule even on holidays and weekends.

Switch off all your electronic screens at least one hour before your bedtime – The blue light that emits from tablets, phones, TVs, and computers make you feel wakeful as it suppresses the production of sleep-inducing hormones such as melatonin.

Exercise

Sleep is one pillar of brain strength. Physical exercise is another important pillar. Our brains need a continuous supply of oxygen-rich blood for optimal functioning. And what better way to ensure this continuous supply than a good amount of physical exercise? Exercise is the best and the most effective way to drive blood to the brain and improve its functioning.

Physical exercise such as running and jogging triggers the increased production and release of a protein called cathepsin B. This protein, in turn, is responsible for increased neuron growth in the hippocampus area of the brain resulting in new memory connections. Other studies have proven that waiting for about 4 hours after learning a new lesson will help in improved retention and recall capabilities. Here are some brain-boosting tips for your exercise regimen:

- Aerobic exercise is great for your brain as it keeps your blood pumping. Generally, anything that is good for the heart is good for the brain

- If you take a long time to clear out your sleep fog, then exercising in the morning is the best. It not only clears your sleep fog well but also primes your mind for improved learning throughout the day.
- Physical activities with complex motor skills or hand-eye coordination are particularly good for improving brain functioning
- Exercise breaks during the day help clear mental fatigue, especially the post-lunch slump. A short walk is sufficient for brain reboot

Eat Healthily

Trans-fats and saturated fats from red meats are connected to bad memory. Researchers have concluded from various studies that cholesterol can clog your heart as well as your brain. The plaques from cholesterol buildup can lead to damage of brain tissues resulting in a reduced supply of oxygen-rich blood thereby impairing learning and memory.

On the contrary, unsaturated fat-rich diets (typically fruit and veggies, seafood, nuts, olive oil, etc.) are connected to improved memory and cognitive skills. Here are some more diet-based ideas for improved memory:

Get your omega-3 fatty acids – fish is particularly rich in omega-3 fatty acids (which are linked strongly to memory boosting powers). Include a lot of fish such as salmon, mackerel, halibut, tuna, and more 'fatty' fish. Other sources of omega-3 fatty acids include walnuts, seaweed, flaxseed and its oil, pinto and kidney beans, winter squash, etc.

Include a lot of fruit and vegetables – They are full of antioxidants that protect your brain cells from damage. The more colorful the fruit and vegetables are, the richer in antioxidants they are.

Avoid caffeine – Caffeine affects different people in different ways. For some of us, even the morning coffee could have an effect on the night's sleep. Exercise caution when it comes to caffeine, and choose sensibly depending on your body's reaction to it.

Manage Stress Levels

Stress is one of the worst causes of memory problems and other brain-related issues. Chronic stress can destroy and damage brain cells and the hippocampus area resulting in problems associated with new memories and consolidation. Here are some stress-management tips:

- Set yourself realistic expectations and learn to say no when you cannot take on more than what you have on your plate
- Take short relaxing breaks right through the day
- Don't bottle up your emotions; express them openly
- Balance work and leisure sensibly
- Avoid Multitasking; it drains your brain power and results in reduced efficiency

Another effective way to reduce stress is to laugh more. Here are some tips to make sure you increase the laughter and joy in your life:

'Laughter is the best medicine' is an old but timeless cliché, which is good for the memory too. Studies have shown that laughter affects multiple regions of the brain stimulating it much more than other emotional responses. Additionally, jokes and punch lines are creative and listening to them can stimulate your creative thinking ability too. Here are some ways to improve laughter in your life:

Laugh at yourself – One of the most effective ways to convert serious moments in our life is to find something funny in it, and laugh it off. This approach to laughing at the difficult and embarrassing aspects of our life will teach us to look at everything around us with joy, happiness, and laughter.

Move toward laughter – Allow yourself to be attracted by laughter. Whenever and wherever you hear laughter, gravitate toward it and share and laugh about the joke. Sharing something innocently (without rancor or malafide intent to hurt) funny by anybody is an opportunity to laugh.

Surround yourself with happy people – Happiness is contagious and so is sadness. Being around morose and sad people will affect you too. Avoid them as much as you can, or at least, consciously avoid being affected by their depressive attitude. Instead, surround yourself with happy people who never lose an opportunity to laugh.

Pay attention to children's behavior – Children are the most unaffected by the vagaries of life, and what they exhibit is the truest form of emotion that can be seen. Look at children's behaviors and you will notice that they can laugh and find joy in anything around them. Try and emulate them as much as you can.

Make time for your family, friends, and loved ones – If you thought that only serious mental and challenging mental exercises can help you boost your memory, think again. Being around your loved ones in a happy atmosphere is also known to boost memory.

Human beings are social animals. We are not meant to live in isolation. Forget thriving, even surviving in isolation is not easy for us. Relationships, friends, and family stimulate our brains, and human interaction could, perhaps, be the best and the most effective form of mental exercises.

Research studies have proven that strong emotional relationships are not just good for the heart but also for the brain. So, always find time to be amongst loving people who care for and love you. Warm relationships are good for your memory.

More Memory Building Tips

Mnemonics – Remember the school grade mnemonic VIBGYOR to remember the seven colors of the rainbow? Using mnemonics is a powerful tool to remember and recall information from your long-term memory. Here are some examples:

Expression mnemonics or acronyms – **MY VERY EDUCATED MOTHER JUST SERVED US NINE PIZZAS** is a mnemonic that stands for the nine planets in our solar system. The first letter of each word gives the starting letter of the planet's name from Mercury (My) to Pluto (Pizzas). **EVERY GOOD BOY DOES FINE** is an acronym for the treble clef EGBDF (in music).

Music Mnemonics – music can be used to create powerful mnemonics because they are easily repeatable, engaging, and fun. It is so much easier to remember a catchy tune instead of a long string of plain words or texts. Look at all the old school rhymes that you used to learn the alphabets or the song for the elements in the periodic table.

You can create your own song based on a favorite tune. Even the act of creating the song will help in improving your memory through creativity.

Chunking Technique – Another form of mnemonics is to chunk information together. For example, if you have to remember a telephone number like 9995550660, you would most likely say 999 555 0660. This is chunking similar data together thereby increasing your ability to remember.

In the chunking technique, you group similar items together, finding some kind of pattern in them, and then organize them in a way that is logical and structure for easy memory and recall.

For example, in your grocery list, you can group together the times that are found in one aisle. When you are learning history, you can look for connections between the various events during a particular period, and chunk them together.

Chunking techniques work very well because by default our brains look for patterns and connect them together. Our memory works efficiently and effectively to draw information from raw data and find logical patterns by using refined methods of chunking. Here are some examples where chunking techniques will work very well:

- If you have a long list to remember, group similar items together, and form small groups of lists within the big list.
- If the list consists of vocabulary words, then create small groups of similar or related words
- Break your grocery list into fruit list, vegetable list, grain list, dairy list, and so forth.

Make Handwritten Notes of Information – Put away your computer, and revert to making handwritten notes for critical information that you need to remember and recall later on. There are many reasons why handwritten notes are preferable over typing out notes on the computer. Here are some reasons why:

- The act of writing stimulates specific brain cells located at the base and referred to a reticular activating system (RAS). The brain is known to focus more when the RAS is activated. Therefore, when your hand is physically making notes, your brain is more active as it follows the movement of your hand as it forms each letter, which enhances your memory and cognitive skills.
- Research studies have also proven that people who handwrite their lectures are able to deliver them verbatim whereas people who type the lectures out invariably paraphrase the ideas during the class.

So, always try and make handwritten notes as much as possible. Mind maps are useful handwritten notes because you don't have to write long-drawn sentences, and yet, can leverage the advantage of handwriting.

Repetition – How many times have you learned something for a test, and promptly forgotten it almost immediately? Unless we compel our brains to work actively and retained the learned information, we will lose what we have learned. If you want to remember information in the long-term horizon, then you have to vocalize and learn it repeatedly.

Spaced repetition is considered the most efficient way of repeatedly learning. After you have learned something new, you take a short break (2-3 days) and learn it again. Keep increasing this break from 2-3 days to 1-2 weeks to 1-2 months to 6 months as the data gets deeply imbibed into your brain. You can make handwritten notes on flashcards, and use them for this spaced repetition learning.

Conclusion

Learning memory techniques will not just help you pass a test or find your car keys or help you make a grocery list or some such mundane thing. These techniques improve your memory, which has lifelong benefits. With a great memory, you can easily achieve the following:

- Get great grades in school
- Get promotions at work easily because you will be able to recall and follow instructions to the T
- People in sales can do very well with great memory skills as they can recall names of their customers with ease endearing them for life
- Your personal relationships will improve thanks to your ability to remember birthdays, anniversaries, and other important days in the life of your friends and family, and of course, your spouse
- Effects of aging are first felt in the brain. Memory techniques help in staving off the aging process in the brain keeping you mentally sharp and alert even when you are old

Therefore, memory techniques don't just give you productivity and efficiency but also happiness and joy as you learn to live your life in a more fulfilling and meaningful way than before.

Accelerated Learning

Very best way to learn as fast as possible

Improve Your Memory, Save Your Time and Be Effective

By: Lawrence Franz

© Copyright 2018 - All rights reserved.

The contents of this book may not be reproduced, duplicated or transmitted without direct written permission from the author.

Under no circumstances will any legal responsibility or blame be held against the publisher for any reparation, damages, or monetary loss due to the information herein, either directly or indirectly.

Legal Notice:

This book is copyright protected. This is only for personal use. You cannot amend, distribute, sell, use, quote or paraphrase any part of the content within this book without the consent of the author.

Disclaimer Notice:

Please note the information contained within this document is for educational and entertainment purposes only. Every attempt has been made to provide accurate, up to date and complete, reliable information. No warranties of any kind are expressed or implied. Readers acknowledge that the author is not engaging in the rendering of legal, financial, medical or professional advice. The content of this book has been derived from various sources. Please consult a licensed professional before attempting any techniques outlined in this book.

By reading this document, the reader agrees that under no circumstances is the author responsible for any losses, direct or indirect, which are incurred as a result of the use of information contained within this document, including, but not limited to, —errors, omissions, or inaccuracies.

Table of Contents

Introduction 79

Chapter 1: A Quick Introduction to Accelerated Learning 82

Chapter 2: Discovering How Your Brain Learns Best 88

Chapter 3: Before You Start Learning 95

Chapter 4: Accelerated Learning Techniques for the Learning Process 101

Chapter 5: Reviewing After Learning and Tips for Increasing Memory 116

Chapter 6: A Few More Strategies You Can Use to Improve Your Learning Capabilities 135

Conclusion 144

Introduction

One of the most powerful tools that you possess when it comes to achieving success in life is your brain. Your brain controls your abilities; how quickly you think, how rapidly you can learn new material, which tasks get easier with time. Humans use only a small percentage of their brain for thinking. Consider all that you are capable of doing now, did you know that you could do so much more? Simply by training the brain to think and learn faster, you can increase your memory and retention, pick up new topics and perform mental tasks with incredible speed and much more.

Within the brain are an estimated 100 billion neurons and countless synapses. These form connections that let you carry out your daily tasks, from body functions like temperature regulation and breathing to physical actions like typing at the computer or solving a math problem. The more that you use certain synapses, the faster you will find yourself able to learn new things. This happens as the connections in the mind strengthen. Think of the brain as a forest with a walking path that has been treaded through it from frequent use. The more frequently that the walking path is used, the more prominent it becomes.

Oftentimes, if you look up accelerated learning online, you are going to see that there are numerous courses (usually paid) that promise that you and a facilitator or educator will work together to increase your accelerated learning abilities. Other times, accelerated learning describes courses that you can enroll in that take less times than traditional college courses. This makes it hard to find the information you need to tackle accelerated learning on your own. With this book, however, that becomes possible. You will find all the information you need for accelerated learning in one place, without the need to pay for an entire course or work with someone who has their own agenda to think of as well as yours.

This book will be about all the actionable steps that you can take to increase your learning abilities. Through accelerated learning, you will learn how to strengthen the connections in your mind, improving your memory and your ability to retain new information, helping you process information faster, letting you understand new information at a greater capacity, and teaching you how to focus while learning. These skills will give you an unlimited potential for learning, and in turn, an unlimited potential for success.

It does not matter whether you consider yourself young or old—there is never a wrong age to increase your capability for learning! Through accelerated learning, you will find your mind functioning at a level higher than it ever has before.

Best of luck as you begin your accelerated learning journey!

Chapter 1
A Quick Introduction to Accelerated Learning

Before we get started, it's important that you know what the strategies and techniques provided in the following chapters are helping you work toward. It is about more than just being an accelerated learner—developing skills in this area help improve your life and increase your chance of success. This chapter will go over what accelerated learning is and the benefits, so you have a clear idea of the results that you will see as you practice the techniques that follow.

What is Accelerated Learning?

Accelerated learning is simply a rapid way of learning. It describes strengthening those connections in the mind, so you can learn new material and access previously learned material faster. This all serves the overall goal of increasing your abilities in life, putting you ahead of the pack and increasing your brain power so you have a greater chance of success in life.

Something that must be noted is that accelerated learning is not necessarily always about speed. The techniques that you will find in the pages that follow are going to take time to carry out. There are preparations for the learning process, intensive studying sessions, and daily reviews that have to be followed to help you retain information. Even so, this is accelerated learning. By following the guidelines provided in this book, you will find your mind able to recollect information more quickly. Even though the studying sessions seem like they take a lot of work, the work is necessary to commit the things you are learning to memory. This is true accelerated learning—because once those things are committed to memory, you can move on to learning the next topic. Accelerated learning never stops—it is a lifestyle. Fortunately, it is a lifestyle that has unlimited potential to change your life for the better.

Benefits of Accelerated Learning

Time is valuable. When you have spent money on this book (or any courses), it can be hard to commit to the necessary work without a clear picture of what you are going to reap from it. Fortunately, accelerated learning is a skill that can offer benefits in all areas of life.

#1: Retain Useful Information

Have you ever been in a social situation that quickly became awkward when you couldn't remember the other person's name? Or perhaps you have come up with a great idea, but you couldn't put it into words because you couldn't remember the name of the technique that you needed to tweak to do more research and make the solution fit to the problem. When you cannot retrieve the information that you have, life is just more difficult. You have to do more work and your find yourself in situations that could have been avoided if you could have retained certain information.

#2: Stop Forgetting Responsibilities

When you lead a busy lifestyle, it is all too easy to forget what you need to accomplish. For example, your boss may assign you certain tasks over the weekend when they see you in passing. If you cannot remember all those tasks when it comes time to do them, you may face consequences for not completing the work. Accelerated learning helps you remember what you need to be doing, so you don't forget to complete projects, attend meetings or dates, or make it to other appointments again.

#3: Reduced Risk of Alzheimer's and Other Degenerative Diseases

Even in healthy people, the natural decline of the brain's age and abilities can begin in the 20s. This marks the end of puberty and growth, thus, the end of the period when the brain is at its peak. For some people, this just means that their mind needs to focus more to get the same results—they need brighter lights for reading or music needs to be louder for them to experience it. For others, however, this naturally occurring process eventually results in a neurodegenerative disease like Alzheimer's, Parkinson's, Huntington's, and frontotemporal dementia.

Though there is still speculation as to what exactly the cause and cure for neurodegenerative diseases is, it is apparent that the people who have the greatest mind health in their later years of age are those that continued learning. This is because continuing to learn, especially through practicing accelerated learning, improves the connections in your mind and helps prevent neurodegenerative disease.

#4: Better Problem Solving

Knowing information and knowing how to apply it are entirely different things. For example, you may have read an article on how to change the oil in a car, but have never seen a diagram or been under the hood of a car. The problem is that without the ability to identify the different parts of the engine and what you need to do with the oil, having the knowledge is not enough.

Accelerated learning is not just about taking in as much knowledge as you can. It helps you think and analyze critically, giving you the ability to problem solve. This is helpful in work settings where problem solving is necessary to meet the demands of your job, but it is also useful in life.

#5: Greater Chance of Success

When you practice accelerated learning, you are giving yourself a competitive edge over those who are happy enough once they receive their education. Some people graduate from high school or college, settle into a job, and decide that they are not going to work toward any more mental improvement in their life. Sadly, these people often do not reach anywhere near a level of success that they can live comfortably and provide for the future generations of their children and grandchildren.

Accelerated learners keep their minds sharp. They can think critically and rationally, solve problems, and uncover and learn new information that keeps them ahead of other people in their field. This gives them a leg-up that can translate to promotions, new opportunities, and overall a higher level of success.

Chapter 2
Discovering How Your Brain Learns Best

One of the problems noted with what could be considered 'traditional' schooling is that the large class sizes do not allow teachers to account for all the students' best learning abilities. There are four major classifications of learning styles, including visual, auditory, tactile/kinesthetic, and reading/writing. This chapter will explain these and provide insight into what you should do to make accelerated learning easier for yourself. As you read, think about the common practices listed for each type of learner to determine which type of learner you are. There are also tests that you can take to determine this information if you are unsure.

Visual Learning Preference

People who have a visual learning preference prefer to see things when they are learning, including words on a page, demonstrations of what they are learning, or graphic charts. Visual learning is highly common, with around 60% of students saying that they prefer visual learning. Some common habits of visual learners include:

- Being distracted by action or movement, but less likely to be distracted by noise
- Learn well through descriptions (rather than pictures)
- Learn easily through visual demonstrations
- Recognize words by sight
- Tend to forget names, but remember faces
- Organize thoughts with lists

Auditory Learning Preference

Students that have an auditory preference often work better when hearing things. However, they tend to prefer hearing lectures or listening to books. Some common traits include:

- Being distracted by noise and preferring to learn in a quiet environment
- The ability to remember names, but difficulty visualizing the person unless they are in front of them
- Likes recorded books

- Prefers discussions, dialogues, and plays
- Solves problems through talking them out

Tactile/Kinesthetic Learning Preference

Tactile learners have a preference for touch, as do kinesthetic learners. The major difference is that tactile learners prefer hands-on activities, while kinesthetic learners prefer the use of gross motor skills, like full body movement. Even so, many of the activities that they prefer while learning are very similar. Some habits include:

- Learn best while moving
- Like labs, demonstrations, and projects that require a hands-on approach
- May doodle or make graphic charts to remember information
- Learn better by taking notes
- Have high levels of energy
- May have trouble concentration while sitting and reading material

Reading/Writing Learning Preference

People with this learning preference learn best through reading and writing. They also communicate in the same way and may prefer chatting or sending texts over a voice call. Some common learning habits include:

- Writing out their notes or information they want to remember

- Prefer sitting and reading material (usually alone)

- Re-reading notes before test

- Turning visual charts and graphics into words in your mind

- Communicates more clearly through writing than speaking

- Prefers papers and written assignments to presentations and group work

How to Use This Information

Knowing your learning style should not be something that holds you back. Even if you are an auditory learner, for example, it does not mean that you cannot learn from a hands-on learning technique. In fact, most learners can learn from all four of the categories, but have strengths in certain ones.

The goal with providing this information is that you get greater insight into what works for you. It only makes sense that if you combine your natural learning abilities with new information that you are trying to understand that you will comprehend the information more rapidly. Additionally, this information can be useful if you are having trouble understanding something or if you are working with a difficult topic. You can combine the way that you best learn with the topic you are trying to learn and end up making the road to learning significantly easier.

Accelerated learners often use this information to develop in certain areas as well. For example, even if you have had trouble learning auditory in the past, there are techniques that you can practice for improving your auditory learning abilities. This will give you a greater range of inputs for learning new information.

The Real Goal: Learning How to Make Each Learning Style Work for You

It is true that you should focus on your strengths, especially when you are working with a difficult topic. However, it is equally important that you learn to develop each of the skills in a way that they can be used to learn information. When you learn information in more than one way, you are giving yourself the opportunity to remember the knowledge in several ways. For example, imagine that you are trying to work out complex math problems. You could listen to a seminar with subtitles, so you could hear and say what the speaker is saying. You could also engage the read/write and kinesthetic techniques by writing out and solving problems using the equations provided. By engaging all the learning styles, you are also increasing comprehension of the topic, so you understand it more deeply and have better ideas of how to apply it in a real-life scenario.

Example of How to Actively Learn Using All the Learning Strategies

Even once you are aware of your strengths, you should not turn your focus completely to that style of learning. Instead, make it a habit to engage all the different styles of learning. For example, when you are watching a seminar, reading information, or reading a book, physically highlighting the information or writing notes can be helpful. If a person is teaching you something, ask for a demonstration to actively engage the senses. If this is not an option, you can also demonstrate the action yourself based on what you have learned so far. It is also useful to take a step back and visualize what you are learning and where it fits into the bigger picture.

You can enhance your auditory learning skills by repeating the ideas out loud or summarizing them for yourself. When you summarize information, it gives you the opportunity to increase your comprehension and to relate it to ideas that you are already familiar with. A way to further your memory is to read it in a way that makes it memorable—say the material with an accent or repeat it in a dramatic way. The key is to be interested and enthusiastic, positive emotions that will trigger the long-term memory center of the limbic system.

When learning in a hands-on way, make it a habit to actively learn what you are reading or seeing. Keep a pen in your hand so you can physically write notes or take action to practice the material. You can also make a game out of organizing the information, using flash cards, matching games, and creating diagrams to help you remember and comprehend information.

Chapter 3
Before You Start Learning

Accelerated learning is not something that you can just jump into. Unlike people who just dive into a topic, people who excel at learning take the time to prepare. Preparation involves things like being in the right environment, reviewing information, and setting learning goals, to name a few things. It puts your mind focus and gives you time to consider what you stand to gain by taking in this new information.

This chapter is organized into steps. It can be very beneficial to carry out these steps as a process that you use each time that you sit to learn something new. It will help your mind focus by making the process a habit, which prepares it for learning each time that you sit down.

Step 1: Setting the Environment

One of the biggest factors in accelerated learning is being able to focus. Even the most intelligent people have trouble learning in a crowded, noisy, or otherwise distracting environment. Ideally, you should choose one area (or a handful of areas) where you regularly return to study.

Something to consider in your environment is seating. You do not want to make it a habit to study slouched over your desk or sitting in your bed. Choose somewhere that you can sit upright, with good posture that will keep the blood flowing freely from the heart to the brain. This will help you stay alert and focused while you are studying.

Finally, be sure that your learning environment is somewhere that you can be away from distractions. The environment should be quiet, without a television going in the background. Try to minimize noises, using a fan or playing quiet music (if it is not distracting to you) to keep out the sounds you cannot control, like the sounds of traffic, trains, or dogs barking, or the sounds of the people you live with.

Don't Forget the Mental and Physical Environment

Have you ever had a migraine and tried to 'tough it out' at work anyway? Or maybe you have worn a pair of pants or shoes that were too tight, causing you to feel uncomfortable. When you are physically uncomfortable or in pain, it becomes that much harder for you to focus on the task at hand. Rather than focusing on learning the material in front of you, your brain will constantly be interrupted by the discomfort or pain that you are experiencing.

Likewise, you also must take care of your emotional environment before you sit down to learn. It is going to be nearly impossible to focus on learning if someone you are close to has just died or if you have had an especially bad day at work.

Before you sit down to learn, be sure that you are as pain-free and comfortable as possible, both mentally and physically. If there are any steps you can take to alleviate the pain a little as you try to learn, take those actions before you sit down. If emotional trauma is the problem you are experiencing, then spending a few minutes meditating to clear your mind beforehand can be very beneficial.

Step 2: Decide (Generally) What You Want to Learn

People often associate learning with school, where they may have struggled simply because they did not enjoy the subjects that were being taught. However, have you ever been in a class that you truly enjoyed? Whether it was science, art, history, music, math, or reading, think about how that class influenced you. Did it seem to make learning more natural? Did you possibly even enjoy yourself?

Enjoyment is a major factor in the learning process. When you are having a good time, your mind is signaling to the limbic system in the brain that it should store long-term memories. This is the reason that it is easier to remember memories that you have a positive relationship with.

This means, however, that you should use accelerated learning as a tool to learn information that you want to learn about. While you can use it for learning other topics, you will find it easier to apply the process to interesting topics. Additionally, you will be more likely to use these topics in day-to-day life, reinforcing what you have learned.

Step 3: Research an Overview of the Topic

There is a reason that school starts with the basics and foundations, and then builds on them to help students understand on a larger scale. Knowledge is always intertwined with other ideas and higher levels of knowledge. Learning is something that has an infinite possibility for improvement. That is the reason that someone who has attended college for eight years has a higher certification than someone who has attended college for four years—because they have a higher level of expertise from learning more about the subject.

Before you sit down to learn something for the first time, take a moment to consider it on a grander scope. Think about how it might apply to something you are interested in learning in the future or how it relates to things you already know. This will help motivate you because understanding the broader scope helps secure the reasoning behind learning the topic in the first place. Take the opportunity to make sure you are focusing on the foundations of the topic before more advanced learning—this will save you a lot of frustration in the future.

Step 4: Set a Learning Goal

Goal setting has been proven through scientific studies to help people reach success. It gives you a clear idea of what you are working toward and motivates you by providing you a clear deadline for your goals. Be clear about exactly what you want to learn and how quickly you want to learn it. Visualize that you must give a class or write a book by your deadline and that there are countless people depending on you to provide them with the knowledge you are supposed to be learning. Be clear about your goal and exactly what you want to learn—the clarity will help you intensify your desire and motivate you to meet your learning goals.

Chapter 4
Accelerated Learning Techniques for the Learning Process

Once you have set a learning goal ad the environment is ready, you are adequately prepared for accelerated learning. As you read the advice provided in this chapter, you will find it is important to remember that accelerated learning is a process. Many of the techniques provided from this point forward are going to seem as if they are time consuming. You may even find that you are taking longer using these techniques than you would otherwise.

Do not become discouraged when you learn the amount of work that is required for accelerated learning. There is no single step that you can take to become an accelerated learner overnight. In fact, it will take weeks or even months before you notice any significant differences. However, the time saving with accelerated learning comes into the picture when you begin to understand information better. You will be able to remember it more quickly and accurately, letting you quickly analyze and adapt to situations and life. By applying these techniques to learning, you'll find that learning does not take as long the more that you practice it. Even complex subjects become easier to learn and understand because your mind is better equipped to carry out this task.

Engage Yourself in Full-Brain Learning

The different areas of the human brain have different responsibilities and roles in the learning process. The left brain is responsible for tasks of reasoning. It is the language center of the brain and is responsible for things like logical think, chronological order, facts, words, and numbers. The right side of the brain is responsible for creative tasks. It plays a role in remembering melodies, images, and symbols, and recognizes spatial relationships and patterns. While the left brain focuses on the information piece by piece, the right brain looks at things as a whole picture. It is responsible for thinking that is of an intuitive or imagistic nature. Finally, the limbic system plays a critical role in long-term memory by deciding what information you forget and which information you remember. Memories that are emotionally appealing, such as those that are positive in nature, are more likely to remembered than memories that have a negative emotional feel.

Have you ever noticed how easy it is to remember the lyrics to song? This is because music engages the left brain with the words and the right brain with the patterns and melodies. The final aspect is emotional appeal—the limbic system decides if the information is important enough to be remembered, depending on how it appeals to the emotions.

People who are accelerated learners retain information better because they engage all three parts of the brain. This is called full-brain learning. Not only does it increase comprehension of a subject, because you are learning it as individual facts and looking at the bigger picture, full-brain learning helps you remember information better. It creates more pathways to the topic, making it easier to recollect.

To engage your brain fully when learning, it is important to involve processes that engage all three of the sections of the brain. A good example of this are learning songs for kids, which teach them letter sounds, how to count, and more. Kids are more apt to remember the song because the lyrics are interacting with the left side of the brain and the music is working with the right side of the brain. Kids' songs are also typically upbeat and positive, which encourages the limbic system to remember the information.

Of course, you are not going to be listening to musical numbers describing the complex topics that you are learning through life. You can still use the same principles to help make learning easier for yourself, though. When you are reading or listening to a lecture on something, try to create images to organize information or look for patterns or relationships to other ideas that you are familiar with. Make it a habit to analyze the individual facts and to look at the larger picture. Being passionate or excited about what you are learning can also be helpful, as this passion translates to a positive emotion that the limbic system is likely to remember.

Setting Your Mindset: Inducing Alpha Brain Waves

In the mind, there are four basic brainwave classifications, each of them having a specific pattern and speed that they follow. Most of the day, people are experiencing beta brainwaves. Beta brainwaves have the highest frequency, being classified as those that are above 12 Hertz. The beta brainwave period is when we are most alert, but it is also the worst time for learning because we are being stimulated by all that is around us. This makes it a time when it is easy to be distracted.

Alpha waves are more relaxed than beta waves. It is easier to concentrate, but you are not so relaxed that you are too tired to focus. Not only are you able to increase concentration, the relaxed state of your mind lets information be received at a much faster rate.

The other two stages are theta waves, which are between 4 and 7 Hertz, and delta waves, which are under 4 Hertz. Theta waves represent deep periods of relaxation and are most common when we are sleeping. Delta waves are extremely slow, being the slowest recorded brainwaves in humans. Delta waves can be associated with deep, healing sleep. Delta waves are not common in adults, but can be seen frequently in infants and young children.

To reach the ideal rate of brainwaves during the learning process, you will need to relax from your awakened state. This is quite easy to do. Go to your learning area and close your eyes. Breathe deeply ten times, slowly inhaling through your nose and exhaling through your mouth. You know you have reached the alpha wave stage when your consciousness feels awakened, but your mind is calm and at peace.

Using Music to Induce Alpha Waves

Not only is music a great way to relax the mind into an alpha wave state, it can help you retain more of the information you are learning. Alpha waves are generally associated with a calm, peaceful, and generally pleasant feeling. If you listen to music without vocals, it also has potential to stimulate the right side of the brain in addition to the limbic system. This will engage all three parts of your brain when you are studying material.

Passive vs. Active Music

There are many mind-expanding music forms available, each of them designed to sync up with your mind and produce certain brainwaves. However, this is not the only type of music that can be beneficial to learning. Studies carried out at Irvine University showed a correlation between musical influence and cognitive tasks that required mental imagery.

The ideas uncovered were a type of music hypnosis, which was most effective when combining relaxation and music. It is not always a matter of having active or passive music, however. The research that was carried out tested for these anomalies, but it was found that there was no significant difference in student abilities according to which type of music they listened to.

Something that can be noted from these studies is the importance of mental imagery to the learning process, especially if you are to engage all sides of the brain. The musical connection can help channel positive emotions, while the imagery engages the right side as well as the logical thoughts from the left.

Get in the Habit of Taking Breaks

If you talk to people about the secret to success, most will tell you that it is hard work. However, people who are truly successful do not push themselves to their breaking point, instead valuing an increased capacity for thought and better mental health. When you are learning something new, taking a break is not a bad thing. In fact, taking a break after studying information is critical to retaining it.

Your brain cannot actively store and organize information when you are focusing its attention on learning new material. Make it a habit to work for 20-30 minutes and then take a five-minute break. You should use the five-minute break to go for a walk or get a cup of coffee, something that you do not need to engage the active thinking processes of the mind to do. During this time, your mind will take the information that you have learned in the last 20-30 minutes of your study session and store it away.

Another benefit of taking regular breaks is that it coincides with the natural human attention span. Even the most focused people can have trouble concentrating for long periods of time. Once you are out of a natural zone of focus, the difficulty you experience concentrating makes learning an inefficient process. You are actually saving time by taking a break, rather than losing it, because you will learn at a more rapid rate once you return to your studies.

Take Notes the Right Way

Have you ever frantically scribbled during a lecture, only to find yourself behind of the speaker's voice and unable to understand what they are talking about because you were focused on note taking and missed critical information? This is a common problem among students, especially those who have not mastered paraphrasing or shorthand.

The ability to paraphrase is one of the first tools that accelerated learners should focus on. Paraphrasing means taking information that is given to you and putting it into your own words. It is describing a word or phrase without copying it, forcing you to think critically about what the information is trying to say and helping you think more deeply about the meaning behind it.

If you truly cannot keep up, even when paraphrasing, you will need to find a solution that lets you slow down and take notes. However, most teachers are not going to slow down for their lectures—their goal is to make sure they can educate students within the given time period. One option is to learn shorthand. Shorthand simply describes using abbreviations and symbols for words. These abbreviations and symbols serve the purpose of holding the place of a certain word. When you go back to look at the notes later, you will recognize this word. However, you will be able to write more a shorter period of time because you are writing out less letters.

Rewriting notes and reciting them out loud are two ways that you can help commit the information from your notes to memory. In some cases, summarizing the learning material according to its importance can help you spatially or chronologically organize the information, giving you greater insight into how it fits into the bigger picture. This also helps you analyze the topic at a deeper level.

Once you have practiced several times, number the notes and try to recreate them on a separate piece of paper. If there are any you forget, mark them to be looked over again later. While you are organizing the notes, you will find that it is useful to find a way to create groups, sequences, or lists with the information. By labeling these lists with an appropriate keyword, you are assigning them a trigger that will make it easier for you to recollect the information when it is necessary.

Creating Mind Maps

Mind maps are designed to organize information in a way that makes it easy to understand, easy to learn, and easy to remember. After studying a topic, create a mind map by writing the main topic in the center of the paper. From the center of the paper, the mind map is going to branch out into different categories. This is similar to the 'trigger' or 'title' words that you would use when creating lists of information. The title words should consist of words that describe larger categories, with the goal of breaking the information down like you would an outline.

Once you have written out the different categories, you are going to choose keywords that represent the information you have learned. There should be several keywords for each title category, branched out around them. The key to choosing the perfect keyword is selecting one that relates to an entire idea, letting you recollect the information even though you have not written out every single detail.

As you are creating the mind map, it can be helpful to use different shapes and colors to represent the different levels. By using shapes and colors, you are engaging the visual senses and the creative side of your brain. Adding pictures and symbols is another options. Try to use bright or 'happy' colors—remember that positive mental association is important if you want to engage the limbic system in the learning process.

After you have created a mind map, you will need to commit the ideas to memory. One of the best things to do is to look the information over and then put it away. Try to recreate the map from memory. When you are finished, you are going to compare it against the original. This gives you insight into your problem areas and the topics that you need to work on committing to memory more. You should do this several times until you can fully complete the memory map—this signifies that your mind has committed it to memory completely.

One of the great things about mind maps is that you do not have to limit your use of them to committing information to memory. Mind maps can also be used as an alternative to a traditional outline in the writing process, a tool that can help students who do not do well with the rigid, formal structure of an outline. They are also useful for planning, problem solving, setting goals, preparing speeches, and conducting other types of creative work.

Memory Trees

Memory trees are best used for condensing and understanding information when you are reading a book or other lengthy material. It helps you summarize on a smaller level, giving you pieces that you can look to instead of just the overall picture. This helps you collect bits of data to build a foundation before you consider how the material works as a whole.

When you are first starting, it might be easiest to summarize by paragraph. Use one sentence to define each paragraph and write it down on a page. Do this until you have completed the material—you'll find that you have an incredibly accurate and detailed summary of what you have read. Over time, you will find that you can summarize an entire page, rather than going by paragraph. This will not be quite as detailed, but it will sufficiently summarize what you have just learned. You should think of these as the individual leaves of the tree, the smaller bits of information that branch off from the main source (the trunk).

Once you have summarized all the pages in a chapter, turn to a new page and write one sentence that summarizes that chapter. This part represents the branches of tree—there will be significantly less tree branches than leaves. Additionally, the branches support the leaves because they summarize them all as a whole. Once you have finished this step, you should be left with a list of main idea 'branches.'

Finally, you will reach the trunk of the tree. The trunk of the memory tree should be one or two sentences that summarizes all that you have just learned. The major benefit of working in this way is that each time you review the information on the tree to summarize it, you are repeating it and committing it to memory. Creating a memory tree also clearly shows you the connection between the different ideas presented in the material that you just learned.

Telling a Story with the Information

Have you ever tried to remember a seemingly unrelated list of words? Maybe you are studying for a vocabulary test or maybe you need to remember some key points for a presentation.

The best way to practice this is to get a list of ten words and create a story with them. Here's an example.

Tomato

Clown

Mother

Run

Chair

Stretcher

Rock

Laughter

Red

Lion

A bright, red TOMATO is placed on a CLOWN's face. The clown pulls off the tomato and looks at it, his red nose in one hand and the tomato in the other. He turns and throws the tomato at your MOTHER. Shocked, mother starts to RUN through the aisles of the theater, only to trip over a CHAIR that has been placed in exactly the wrong place.

Confused as to if it is part of the act or if mother is injured, two paramedics walk over with a STRETCHER. Realizing that there is a risk mother may be hurt, they ask her to sit down so they can wheel her over to be looked at. The wheel of the stretcher hits a ROCK and tips over, as the crowd roars with LAUGHTER, assuming now that it must be part of the act.

Mother turns RED with anger, sputtering at the paramedics and the crowd continues to roar with laughter, much like the roar of the LION that has just entered the ring to steal away the crowd's attention.

Each of the words in the list seemed unrelated, but the story brought them together. By remembering the information using a story, you are creating vivid imagery that helps you connect the words. This can be useful for test taking, remembering to-do lists, and more.

Chapter 5
Reviewing After Learning and Tips for Increasing Memory

Have you ever heard the phrase, "If you don't use it, you lose it?" This can be applied to things like working out and muscle mass, but also applies to matters of the brain. When you do not use information for a long period of time, it becomes harder to recollect. Eventually, you may even find that it is impossible to bring the information to the forefront of your mind at all.

The key to overcoming the 'use it or lose it' conundrum is to regularly review the information you are learning. It is important to remember to go back to the basics and address the foundations of what you are trying to build on. Additionally, you can strengthen the usefulness and improve how easily you access the information by applying it to situations that arise in daily life. This chapter will go over the best techniques to do this.

Ideal Schedule for Review

One of the reasons that people cite for letting themselves lose all the information that they have learned is a lack of time. They are so focused on the future and continuing to expand their knowledge that they do not want to commit the few short minutes that are necessary for regular review.

Keep in mind that it only takes a few minutes of your time to review for the several hours that you have spent studying. If you were to forget the information and need to learn it again, all the hours you have worked on it have been wasted. Rather than wasting these hours, it is best to follow a schedule and to review for a few minutes on this schedule:

- Review daily for the first week and while you are still learning the materials at the end of each study session

- Review the material one-week later, reading the summaries and looking over any graphic organizers you may have created

- Review the material one month later, reading over the notes and then testing to see if you remember the information

- Review the material six months later, giving yourself a few moments to review before testing to see if you can recollect the information

If you make a habit of reviewing the information you have learned and revisiting it, even months down the road, you are going to get yourself in the habit of retaining information. By doing this, you can expect to be capable of remembering at least 80% of the material six months after you have learned it. If you do not study, however, the research shows that the mind loses an average of 70% of the material that was studied after six months.

Keep a journal where you write down all your notes and information. This information should be dated, so that each day, you can review the relevant information. Every day, you should review what you learned in the previous day, one week ago, one month ago, and six months ago. This lets you regularly review information, without having to dedicate a large chunk of time to it. You should only be reviewing a minute or two for each hour that you spent learning the subject.

As you are reviewing, if you find that you forget material, commit it to memory by creating a mind map, memory tree, or other graphic to help you store the information in your mind again. This will be necessary sometimes to continue on your accelerated learning path.

Applying What You Have Learned

Aside from reviewing knowledge just so you have it, you can review what you have learned every time that you use it in daily life. Accelerated learning is something that you should use to study something you are passionate about, so it is likely something that you can involve in your day-to-day activities.

General Applications for Learning Material

In cases where you may be learning something for your personal enjoyment or to use in your dream career later in life, it is still important to find a way to apply what you have learned if you do not want to use it. Reviewing can be helpful, but you should take steps to apply the information as well. For example, you can create a mind map from memory or explain to someone what you have learned using your own words.

Finding ways to practice the information is essential to building confidence. Confidence is a positive emotion that you can use to help trigger the limbic brain to store information as long-term memories. Once they are stored, reviewing them will let you access them whenever you need to. Continue to put effort forward into practically using what you have learned. With time, your goal should be to master it.

Increasing Memory Retention

Humans only use a small percentage of their brain. Even the most intelligent people like Stephen Hawking and Albert Einstein used just a small percentage of their brain. This leaves most of the brain cells in the mind untapped, ready to receive and store new information but with people not having the capacity to remember nearly that amount of information.

Memory retention, however, has less to do with the number of brain cells available and more to do with association. Before your mind can retrieve a memory, there must be something that triggers it to remember. The key, therefore, is creating associations in the mind. There are three essential parts to developing a tremendous memory, including association, imagination, and location.

As we learn new information, it is critical to associate it with the things that we already know. This creates a bridge between information that we have already memorized and the new information. It is this connection that lets us access this information later. After creating associations, you also must find a way to make the information meaningful to you. Information that is meaningful is more likely to be stored in the long-term memory, especially when the associations that you have with the subject are positive.

Imagination plays a large role in making the information that you have learned more concrete. Visual associations are especially helpful, as they can be paired with words to form the connection in the left and right hemispheres of the brain. By using your imagination to turn dull, lifeless topics into those that are colorful and meaningful, you end up with memorable representations that can easily be recollected.

Location is also key. The location does not describe where you were when you learned the information—it describes where the information is stored in the mind. You must find a way to recollect the information by creating associations to that specific location. For example, if you are trying to remember the activities that you did yesterday, you would first have to locate the area of the mind where you stored information about the places that you went the day before. Once you remember the places you went, you will be more likely to remember what you did.

Visualization and Concretization

Whoever said, 'A picture is worth a thousand words' might be on to something. The mind is known for remembering images at a much better rate than words, which is the reason that associating the things that we learn with objects or pictures can help you recollect them. The key to doing this is being specific when you visualize the object, which makes it concrete. This concreteness, paired with visualization of an image, creates a strong connection in your mind that will make it easier to remember when you are ready to recall the information.

The first step is to choose an image that correlates to a concrete thought. For example, imagine that you are trying to commit your grandmother's pumpkin pie recipe to memory. You may imagine the recipe printed on a piece of paper that is attached to a pumpkin, relating it with the concrete words of 'pumpkin pie.' Once you have made this simple relationship in your mind, you are going to take steps that will make the visualization memorable.

In the example of the pumpkin pie, you can make the memory vivid by remembering how the pie tastes so that when you taste the filling, you know if you have left an ingredient out. You can also make it active and meaningful, by remembering the times that you have spent in the kitchen making pumpkin pies with your grandmother. Making the memory interesting can also help— maybe you can think of something funny that happened one time when you added the wrong ingredient to the pie or your grandmother's bizarre behavior. However you try to do it, the goal is to create a strong link to your memory. You can do this in several ways, including:

- Making the memory vivid- Engage as many of the five senses (sight, smell, touch, sound, and taste) as you can and visualize how each of them plays a role in the scenario.

- Making the memory active- Try to involve movement in your visualization, picturing yourself doing the activity when it is possible. If movement is not possible, consider animation or having your learning material interact with something else. The key is to bring it to life in some way.

- Make the memory interesting- Adding an interesting element to the material you are going to learn is what is going to engage the emotional response from the limbic system and create the positive association stand out. Find a way to add positive emotion, humor, or exaggeration to the material. You could also visualize something that is dramatic, bizarre, bright, colorful, unusual, or otherwise amusing.

- Make the memory meaningful- The other way to evoke a positive emotional response is to give the material meaning. If you are pursuing the material because it is a topic you have always wanted to learn about or because it will help you get into your dream job, you are more likely to have that positive association and meaning. When you do not have that organize the information and images using logic, structure, and patterns.

The Journey Method

One of the things that famous fictional detective Sherlock Holmes is known for is his 'mind palace.' He uses patterns and logic to uncover information. To make this information useful, however, Sherlock stores vast amounts of memories and information in his mind. This gives him a superior mind, as well as the 'powers' that he uses to deduce the answer at crime scenes and learn more about people. He is not psychic—

he has simply trained his mind to rapidly access and analyze the memories and information that he has at his disposal.

The journey method is much like Sherlock's mind palace. This powerful technique will let you rapidly memorize information and recollect entire series of facts. You achieve these capabilities by creating 'routes' between the different facts and figures in your mind. You take your mind on a journey, training it to travel to different locations in your mind. This works because it is significantly easier for the mind to remember routes and locations than it is to remember seemingly unconnected facts and images.

You should start with a journey that has about ten steps, or ten pieces of information. With time, you will be able to process hundreds or thousands of steps at a time. As you adapt to the technique, however, it is best to keep things simple. The first thing you should do is choose a significant location for your journey. For Sherlock, he referred to his journey as a mind palace.

For example, imagine that you are passionate about survival skills and you are trying to learn about edible plants. Start with a list of ten plants that you are familiar with. You should know how to identify them, but also what their name is and what they taste like (if you have the opportunity to look for and try these edible plants). The journey for this might take you through the woods or on a walk through your local park. Stop at ten different intervals on your journey, imagining that you come to a cluster of one of the edible plants at each interval. As you visualize the different plants, be as specific and detailed as possible. Engage all the senses and make the stop interesting, making it worth memorizing to your mind.

Sequence is important when you are on these journeys, so it is important that you visualize it that you memorize it the same way each time. Your mind journey should make logical sense. When trying to memorize the edible plants, for example, you might want to consider the plant that has the most nutrition or the one that is most easily available first. Visualize the steps of your journey several times over, being careful to go into great detail every time.

As you master the mind journey with ten steps, you will find that you are ready to create other journeys within your mind. These journeys may have hundreds or thousands of steps. There is really no limit to the number of mind journeys that you can create since you can use any location that you know well to store information. You might use different areas of your house, the local beach, the supermarket, or any other place that you are familiar with. When you run out of physical locations in your life to use, you can also turn to imaginary settings like those from games, books, movies, or stories for storing information.

How to Put This into Practice

Once you have a group of related information that you want to learn, the first step is to create a logical list of the facts. Write down all the keywords that you need to associate with the information. Think of a concrete image (like the way that the edible plant looks) that you can associate with the keyword and write it down. Recording the order is important because it keeps you on track until you have the information memorized.

With each step through the 'park' you have visualized, you are going to encounter another small box of these edible plants beside the sidewalk. Each of these will have its own appearance and be labeled with the name. You will imagine the way that the plant smells or tastes when you can.

Something else to note is that you can combine the visual images at different locations so that there are two or more ideas represented by a single location. If you do this, however, it is important that the ideas in the same location are closely linked. Once you have created your list of the location(s) you are visiting and the corresponding images, you are ready to start your journey. Imagine that you are walking alongside or flying above the individual 'stops' on your journey and vividly visit each as you go. After you have done this a few times, imagine yourself flying high above the area and survey the entire journey as a whole, as if you are looking down at the scene from above.

One of the great things about journey maps is that you can use them to learn anything that you can organize. Whether what you need to remember is as simple as a to-do list or as complicated as the entire periodic table, by using a set location, you can greatly increase your capacity to remember the information when you need it to be available.

Be Patient - Mind Journeys Are Complex to Learn

Something to note is that the mind journey method is one that takes time to learn. As you are creating and learning the different steps of your journey, especially as you start to memorize larger numbers of steps, the process will be slow at fast. You are not going to learn to travel deep into your mind palace within seconds the way Sherlock does overnight. However, you will notice that the more you return to your mind journey, the faster you will be able to locate and recollect information.

Memory Room

An alternative to the journey method of recalling information is the memory room. Rather than organize information so you create a journey to reach it, you will take the organized information and store it away in a certain room. This method is useful if you can think of the mind as a library, filled with many rooms and each of them containing a different data set. It also works better for information that is not necessarily chronological, when the order does not really have any significance.

The goal is to imagine a room in detail, either one that you have created (and can remember vividly) or a room that you are familiar with. There should be pictures, shelves, and other areas in the room that are filled with objects and images that correlate to the ideas that you are trying to remember. Each room should be dedicated to a single broad topic, but the information contained in the room does not necessarily have to be in a certain order.

Ideally, you should try to draw out the room and where each of the objects/images are positioned and what they mean. By doing this, you will give yourself a point of reference, so you can ensure there is consistency as you are trying to commit the room to memory. If you find that you need more room after the fact, you can create extensions or hallways that lead to other rooms with related information.

Once you are ready to remember the room, imagine yourself walking down a hallway. This should be a familiar hallway or at least one that you consistently recognize to be associated with your memory room. Stand outside the door for a moment and then visualize yourself pulling it open, accessing the information inside. As you look around the room, the objects and images that you have placed there should remind you of the information you have stored there.

The Peg System

If you must remember short lists of items or numbers, the peg system is ideal. Usually, it is used to remember a list that is as long as ten items, but no longer. The idea is to associate the numbers 0-9 with symbols or images that we see in daily life. The symbol or image that you use will be used to relate to new information that you are going to learn and you are going to combine that symbol with a symbol that represents what you are trying to learn. For example, imagine that you have a list of the ten most popular sports and tennis is the third on the list. You have associated a snowball with the third number. You would imagine that you are hitting the snowball with the tennis racket to imagine it as the third item and remind you that tennis is on the list.

The peg system can also be used to help you remember a short series of numbers, like appointments, dates, measurements, codes, birthdays, and telephone numbers. Imagine for a moment that you develop the peg system as follows:

- 0- balloon with string
- 1- elephant
- 2- snowball
- 3- boomerang
- 4- tree
- 5- butterfly
- 6- candle
- 7- sailboat
- 8- duck
- 9- carrot

Imagine that your sister's birthday is on the 9th day of January, or 1-9. To remember this, you might visualize an elephant eating a carrot. Once you develop a peg system that you use consistently, you will find that referencing the images you create is significantly easier.

Advice for Remembering Names

Some people are great at remembering names, but not faces. Other people can remember faces, but struggle with names. Those who use this accelerated learning technique, however, find themselves better equipped to match faces to names. This can help make a great first, second, and third impression builds relationships and prevents awkward social interactions.

One of the reasons that people often do not remember others' names is because there is a stigma about judging others. They may not look too closely at their facial features or their body as a whole, because they are worried about it seeming as if they are staring or checking the other person out. However, overcoming this awkwardness and taking the chance to look at someone's facial features is far from creepy or awkward.

When you meet someone for the first time, listen closely as they tell you their name. Look them in the eye and in that moment, look at the shape of their face and the details of their eyes and eyebrows. As you converse with them, observe their hair, nose, and mouth. You should also look at their entire body, helping yourself create a mental picture of them. The key is to find distinguishing features—things that set them apart from the mental pictures that you have of your family members and friends in your mind.

Once you have gotten a good look at the person's face, you are going to work to relate their name to their face. Repeat their name at least six times in your mind as you converse with them, helping you commit their distinguished features and the name that goes along with those features to memory. Imagine that the person has their own name written across their forehead, creating a mental image of who they are. Relating someone's name to their features becomes even easier if you know someone who shares their name. For example, if your best friend's name is Jordan and you have a new coworker named Jordan, you can imagine the two of them working together and it will help you create that relationship between the new person's appearance and the name Jordan.

The final thing that you must do is commit to remembering the other person's name.

Oftentimes, people do not remember names because they do not make a conscious effort to commit the name to memory. They assume they will know later or that they will not see the other person again. Instead, get in the habit of trying to remember the names of each person that you meet. Remind yourself that by remembering their names, you may give yourself an advantage in social or work situations in the future.

Chapter 6
A Few More Strategies You Can Use to Improve Your Learning Capabilities

Though traditional, accelerated learning courses focus only on the things you can do while learning, there are several other techniques that can be applied to accelerated learning. Scientists and researchers are always looking for something to advance the learning process, whether it is new tools that can be used or through developing a deeper understanding of the human mind. This chapter will provide you with a few extra tips to help improve your learning practices, so you find yourself able to analyze, store, comprehend, and remember information in a more efficient way.

Neurogenesis

It is true that in general, as we age, we lose brain cells. This can happen over time from lifestyle choices, the foods we eat, environmental circumstances, and any other number of factors. The most recent research on the brain, however, shows that there is a potential to grow new brain cells. Two ways that you can do this is through learning new things and exercising.

Learning Something New

Generally, the focus of learning is either to re-instill your abilities in the basics or to build upon knowledge that you already have. However, one way to advance your learning capabilities is to learn something completely different than anything you have learned previously. Learning something that is entirely new creates new connections in the brain, which you can then use to form stronger neural pathways when creating relationships between other pieces of information.

For example, something like learning a new language teaches much more than just a new way of speaking. It gives your brain a different way to express how you are thinking and feeling. This exposure teaches you a new way of thinking, as well as speaking. Learning an instrument is another good example. It teaches you how to translate from the visual eye to physical activity, by requiring you to read sheet music and translate it before playing the instrument.

Even something like dancing can improve neural pathways in the brain. There is even science to prove this one—several studies have shown that seniors who take up dancing as a hobby are less likely to develop Alzheimer's disease.

Use Your Body to Improve Your Mind

Exercise has many benefits, especially physically and for long-term health. What less people know is that exercising the body can also improve fitness of the brain, by booting memory functions and information processing. Additionally, the research shows that regular exercise helps your mind create neural pathways for learning and accessing new information at a more rapid rate. The final ingredient in the equation is the blood pumping through the body and flowing more easily into the brain. This increases your alertness along with your learning capabilities.

You might be thinking that exercise is just another timely commitment that will interrupt your way of living life. However, the type of exercise required to boost brain function is minimal, especially when you compare it to the time you spend each day learning new information and committing it to memory. Fortunately, the amount of daily exercise that is required to see these benefits is just twenty minutes. Even something like power-walking around the block with your dog can help boost your learning abilities.

Form Meaningful Relationships in Your Life

The meaningful relationships that you form in life may be just as important as the meaningful relationships that you form between the different topics you are trying to understand. When you spend time with the people that you care about, it helps you think more clearly. It is an exercise in learning and understanding a difficult topic because it can be a struggle to see someone else's perspective. When you learn to master things like empathy and compassion, you will find that your ability to see new perspectives also increases.

People who are extroverted, or outgoing, often require social interaction to feel like the best versions of themselves. Extroverted people tend to turn their focus outward, while introverted people tend to turn their focus inward. This leaves introverted people better equipped to understand themselves. Extroverts, on the other hand, often use other people as an outlet to describe and analyze their own feelings.

Add the Right Foods to Your Diet

If you browse the pharmaceutical market for certain 'brain-boosting' supplements, you will likely find that there are numerous blends of ingredients, each of them promising to benefit the way that you think, learn, and remember information. Unfortunately, many of these supplements are based on a limited sample of evidence. The FDA also does not regulated supplements, so there is no guarantee of truth in their claims. There is also no regulation as to the research that must be conducted. Many of these supplements do contain brain-boosting ingredients, but they are not necessarily provided in the amount that they can produce the effects you are looking for.

One food that can boost brain function is dark chocolate. Dark chocolate sends signals to the brain to increase dopamine production, which can improve memory and help you learn faster. Dark chocolate also has antioxidants and flavonols, both of which have been studied and proven to improve overall brain functioning. Including other foods with antioxidants and flavonols can also be beneficial, including 'superfoods' like blueberries, apples, pomegranates, cranberries and others.

There is also a significant amount of research that shows Omega-3 fatty acids are beneficial to brain health. Avocados, seafood like fish, seeds, and nuts are all good sources of Omega-3s. Consuming these healthy fats helps improve the function of the brain. One of the most important is docosahexaenoic acid or DHA. DHA is often given to pregnant and nursing mothers, to help their babies improve cognitive abilities. This is because DHA is the principle fat that makes up gray matter in the brain. Additionally, DHA is known for activating the dorsolateral prefrontal cortex, which is the area of the brain that is associated with memory.

Guided Meditation for Accelerated Learning

To partake in accelerated learning, it is critical that you are in the right mindset for accelerated learning. Your mind is not always open and receptive to the ideas that you try to put into it, especially in times of distraction, pain, or stress. When you simply cannot focus on the task at hand, listening to guided meditation is another way that you can help yourself get into the right mindset for learning.

Guided meditation is simply meditation that is performed while listening to a voice, either someone else's voice or a recording of your own words that you playback. You will use breathing to sink yourself into meditation as you would normally as you start to play the tape, trying to relax your mind and give the words you are hearing power over what you are thinking. Below, you will find an example of a guided meditation for accelerated learning, in case you decide to make your own tape to listen to. If you do record your own tape, then be sure to do it in a calm, unwavering voice. The ellipses represent pauses in speech, where you should pause for a few seconds before continuing on to the next line.

Close your eyes and take a deep breath, inhaling it and releasing it ever so slowly...

As you release this breath, release all the tension in your body and mind... release deeper until you start to enter a learning state...

Allow this learning state to let you remember a simpler time, a time when learning was enjoyable and easy... think back to when learning was so easy that you thought there was no possible way someone couldn't 'get it'...

Now... think of that memory... were you riding a bicycle? Playing a sport or a board game? Were you learning a new subject in school?

Think of a time when learning was simple... and consciously will yourself to go back there... now...

Let yourself exist in that early memory, when learning was so easy... Remember all that you heard, felt, and saw... Re-experience that time as if it is brand new and you are re-living it in great detail...

Take the time now to walk yourself through that event, second by second... Remember everything in great detail...

Now, focus for a moment... How did you feel as learning was so easy that it was almost effortless? Focus on that feeling until it becomes clear and strong... When it is clear, slowly touch your thumb and index finger together...

When the feeling subsides, you can release your two fingers...

Now, go back to another moment when learning was so easy that it was effortless... Feel that moment and re-live it, experiencing the moment in great detail...

Once you can focus on that feeling again, concentrate on it until it is all that fills your mind... let that ease and pleasure of learning fill you... then touch your middle finger to your thumb...

As the feeling subsides, release once again... take another moment to re-live another positive learning experience... remember when it was so easy to learn that it was effortless, quick, and enjoyable... take the time to re-live this moment, experiencing the sounds, feelings, and sights in that time...

As you hone in on that feeling of ease and enjoyment in learning, touch your ring finger to your thumb… continue to hold them until the feeling subsides…

Now… take a deep breath and touch all three fingers to your thumb… focus on how you feel inside… let the ease of learning fill you until there is no room left…

Realize now that you have the power to induce a state of learning… simply by touching your three fingers to your thumb… This signals your ability to enter a state of learning… this signals your ability to open your mind and make it receptive to new materials… Learning is easy… Learning is fun…

Now… awake and become aware of all that is around you… Return now to your work, refreshed and wide awake… Prepared to learn…

The key to this guided meditation is the correlation of the positive feelings of learning be associated with the feeling of your fingers touching your thumb. In the future, your mind is going to associate those positive feelings of learning with that action. With time, you will not need to listen to the guided meditation—you can simply touch your fingers to your thumb to get the desired state of mind.

Conclusion

When you make a commitment to teach yourself accelerated learning, you are committing to a lifestyle and a new way of living. You are opening yourself up to numerous opportunities and benefits. You are taking that first step in building a better life for yourself, one where you can learn what you want and nothing can stand in your way.

Now that you have the information that you need to become an accelerated learner, the only logical step is to put the strategies in this book to the test. With any hope, the ideas presented here have provided you with the actionable steps that you need to take to improve your life for the better.

It is never too late in life to become an accelerated learner and prepare yourself for all the opportunities that life has to offer you. Best of luck as you begin your learning journey!

Speed Reading

The Definitive Guide for Learning How to Read a Book a Day

By: Lawrence Franz

© Copyright 2018 – Lawrence Franz

All rights reserved.

The contents of this book may not be reproduced, duplicated or transmitted without direct written permission from the author.

Under no circumstances will any legal responsibility or blame be held against the publisher for any reparation, damages, or monetary loss due to the information herein, either directly or indirectly.

Legal Notice:

You cannot amend, distribute, sell, use, quote or paraphrase any part of the content within this book without the consent of the author.

Disclaimer Notice:

Please note the information contained within this document is for educational and entertainment purposes only. No warranties of any kind are expressed or implied. Readers acknowledge that the author is not engaging in the rendering of legal, financial, medical or professional advice. Please consult a licensed professional before attempting any techniques outlined in this book.

By reading this document, the reader agrees that under no circumstances are the author responsible for any losses, direct or indirect, which are incurred as a result of the use of information contained within this document, including, but not limited to, —errors, omissions, or inaccuracies.

Table of Contents

Introduction 149

Chapter 1: The True Nature of Speed Reading 150

Chapter 2: Assessing Your Reading Habits 156

Chapter 3: Breaking Bad Reading Habits 164

Chapter 4: Creating Good Reading Habits 172

Chapter 5: Proven Speed Reading Techniques 180

Chapter 6: Creating Your Daily Reading Practice 188

Chapter 7: Some Simple Exercises 197

Conclusion 205

Introduction

Speed reading is a skill that has become highly sought after in recent years. With time becoming an increasingly rare commodity, many people find that they can't read as much as they want to or as much as they were once able to. Furthermore, many work places require that a person becomes familiar with vast quantities of information in a very short amount of time, far faster than conventional reading speeds would allow for. It is for these reasons, as well as many others that more and more people are pursuing the skill set of speed reading. This book will present the various techniques of speed reading, which will teach you how to read more quickly, efficiently and effectively. Not only will these techniques increase your reading speed but they will also increase your ability to obtain and retain information with greater speed and ease. Furthermore, they will teach you how to identify and ignore the vast amounts of fluff and filler that make up the majority of any written material. By the time you finish reading this book, you will be able to improve your reading abilities so that you can read as much as a book a day. In fact, this will be the last book you read the wrong way ever again!

Chapter 1:
The True Nature of Speed Reading

like an expert. This is the true nature of speed reading and the benefits it offers. In order to get the best results from your efforts, it is important to first understand the true nature of speed reading. Most people think of speed reading as the ability to read words at a faster rate. While this is a part of the speed reading process it is not the entirety, nor is it even the most important part. Instead, speed reading is about being able to obtain information contained within a written document at a faster rate. This can be done in several different ways, each focusing on different elements of how to read written material. The bottom line is that speed reading is intended to teach you to know what to read as well as what to ignore. By being able to identify and skip over all irrelevant content you can focus your attention on the words that contain vital information. This allows you to obtain information from any written document in a fraction of the time that it takes most other people. While it may seem as though you are able to read with superhuman speed, the fact is that you simply know how to read

What speed reading isn't

What most people expect to be able to do once they acquire the skill of speed reading is to be able to read upwards of a thousand words per minute, allowing them to breeze through a book like an android. Unfortunately, that goal is simply impossible. One reason for this is that it is physiologically unlikely that you will be able to train your eyes to perceive more than about 500 words per minute. Anything more will significantly reduce your ability to identify the words you see, let alone retain the information they contain. Therefore, while speed reading techniques can significantly increase your reading speed, they can't transform your reading beyond a certain fixed point. That said, the average reading speed is around 200 words per minute, so if you were to increase to the 500 word per minute range, you would reduce the amount of time it takes to read a book by over half.

Another thing that speed reading isn't is a magic wand. You won't find a secret formula or strategy that allows you to suddenly read a text in half the time it would ordinarily take you. Instead, speed reading is a skill that you develop over time with continuous commitment and effort. In a way, it's a bit like weight training. Just as you wouldn't expect to go to the gym for a few sessions and walk out ready for the Iron Man competition, so too, don't expect to achieve maximum speed reading results overnight. While you will be able to see measurable improvement right away, the overall goal will take time to achieve. Only when a person commits to training themselves on a daily basis will they break through the barriers that keep them from reaching their full potential. Therefore, don't expect this to be quick and easy. It will take time and effort, but the results will be more than worth it.

Understanding how things are written

In order to understand how speed reading works you must first understand how things are actually written. More often than not a text will contain far more words than it actually needs to. This isn't for any sinister reason, such as someone trying to hide information within the countless extra words. Instead, it's for better presentation. The truth is that you can express a thought in as little as two or three words, depending on the situation. If you suddenly found yourself hungry, you could simply say "feed me now." Those three words would successfully convey the pertinent information. Unfortunately, they would do so in a way that seemed rude and demanding. Subsequently, you will probably express your feelings of hunger by saying something more along the lines of "I'm feeling pretty hungry all of a sudden. How about we get something to eat?" This sentence is far more conversational and polite, and will doubtlessly be better received. However, it is also five times as long as the original statement, meaning that you took five times the number of words than actually needed in order to get your point across.

Writing does the very same thing. While it's true that you could write a document in such a way as to only use as many words as necessary in order to convey information, such a document would be disjointed, hard to read and fairly boring. In fact, it would probably be like trying to read a phone book. As a result, the average document is written in a way that makes reading it more enjoyable and engaging. Unfortunately, this means that the average document uses far more words than needed in order to convey the information it contains. Speed reading recognizes this fact and addresses it by training the individual to look for information rather than at all of the words a document possesses. Once you learn to look beyond the words, you will be able to obtain the information you need without having to labor through each and every written word in the process. Therefore, rather than reading "I'm feeling pretty hungry all of a sudden. How about getting something to eat?" you will actually be able to see through the words and see the underlying statement "feed me now."

Speed perceiving

When you break down the nuts and bolts of speed reading, you discover that a better term might, in fact, be speed *perceiving*. The main reason for this is that while certain techniques within speed reading will teach you to read words at a faster rate, most will, in fact, teach you to read fewer words altogether. Since most words are only filler, it makes sense to ignore them and focus solely on those words that contain valuable information. This is the essence of speed reading. As you develop the various speed reading skills, you won't be solely fixated on your reading speed. Instead, you will see reading in a whole new light. Sure, there will be times when you will want to read a document word for word, specifically when you are reading for pleasure. After all, poetry simply isn't the same if you skim through it for the pertinent information. And since most works of fiction spend copious amounts of words describing a situation your reading experience will be richer if you take the time and effort to read all of the words.

However, most of the material you read probably won't be for pleasure. Instead, much of it will be for learning specific information and acquiring particular insights. Newspapers are a prime example of this. You really don't need to know all of the sensational details about a particular thing that happened. Simply knowing when, where and how it happened is often enough. Speed reading is the ability to look at a newspaper and take away only the vital information without being dragged down by the countless words used to sensationalize the story. Furthermore, when you master the speed reading skill set you will be able to read business spreadsheets, memorandums, technical data and any other sort of informative document with greater speed, clarity and increased retention. This will make you highly valuable in any business environment. Rather than filling your mind with unnecessary filler and fluff you will be able to pinpoint the pertinent information and move on while others are still meandering through the endless stream of words. This is the true nature and purpose of speed reading.

Chapter 2:
Assessing Your Reading Habits

Before you begin learning the different techniques of speed reading, it is necessary to assess your current reading habits. One of the main reasons for this is that different speed reading techniques are designed to break particular bad habits with regard to reading and replace them with better habits. Therefore, it is important to discover which bad habits you practice regularly in order to ensure that you choose the speed reading techniques that will benefit you the most.

Another reason why it is important to assess your reading habits is so that you can create realistic goals for yourself. If you approach speed reading without a clear idea of what you want to achieve your results will be less measurable and meaningful. Only when you determine how you want to change your reading style can you begin to take the necessary steps toward achieving that goal. Therefore, the first thing you need to do is to closely observe how you read. This includes your reading speed, your eye movements, how easily distracted you are and whether or not you vocalize words as you read them. By recognizing how each of these aspects affects your reading abilities, you will be able to tailor make a specific speed reading regimen that will break your bad habits and provide you with the results you desire.

Determine your reading speed

As mentioned earlier, the average person's reading speed is about 200 words per minute. However, this isn't to say that this is your reading speed. The fact is that each person has a unique reading style, and this style has a direct impact on how many words you are able to read on average. The first thing you need to do, therefore, is to determine your reading speed so that you know where you are in comparison to where you want to be.

There are a few different methods for measuring your reading speed. All of these methods require the use of a timer, however, so it is important that you have a timer available. You can use a stopwatch, a kitchen timer or any other kind of timer that has a bell or an alarm to tell you when to stop. If you don't possess any of these timers you should check your cell phone as just about every cell phone has a timer app. Worst case scenario you can buy a timer for only a few dollars at any grocery store.

Once you have a timer, the next thing to get is something to read. You can use anything at all, including a magazine, newspaper, book or even something online. The important thing is that you are comfortable with whatever it is you are going to read. Once you have your reading material you need to do a word count. You can take the time to count the exact number of words on a page, however, a rough estimate is enough for this exercise. To estimate how many words are on a page simply count the number of words in a single line. Then count the number of lines per page and multiply the two numbers. Thus, if there are 18 words per line and 30 lines per page your estimation would be 30 x 18, which equals 540. The next thing to do is set your timer to either count up or for more time than you will need to read the page. Since the average rate is 200 words per minute you can set your timer for 4 minutes, more than enough time for 540 words. Start your timer and read the page. When you have finished reading stop the timer and see how long you took.

Another way to determine your reading speed is to set a timer for 2 minutes and read as much as you can before the timer goes off. When your time expires you can count the number of words you read and divide by 2 for the number of words you read per minute. This is an easier way to get a precise count of words per minute as you use a precise measure of time rather than a precise number of words. In any event, both methods will allow you to get a sense of your average reading speed, and this is a critical thing to know in order to get the best results when trying to increase your reading speed.

Observe your eye movements

The next thing you need to observe is your eye movements while you read. Most people have the mistaken idea that they simply move their eyes along a line of text at a smooth and steady pace, rarely fluctuating. The truth is that your eye movements are probably quite jerky and irregular, going forward from one group of words to another, and even back again to reread something for clarity or context. Focusing your eyes on a word or group of words is referred to as "fixation." Moving your eyes from one word to another, or from one group of words to another, is called a "saccade." When it comes to speed reading, it is just as important to know how your eyes move as it is to know your reading speed.

Determining your eye movements is a pretty easy process. Simply read one line of text and count the number of times you move your eyes. Be sure to include all movement, including forward, backward and even any time you glance over to something else altogether. Each and every time you move your eyes is important, so be sure to count everything. You can read more than one line of text if you want, however reading one is enough to get an idea of how much time and energy you waste moving your eyes unnecessarily.

The next step is to classify your eye movements. If your count revealed that you moved your eyes eight times while reading a line of text you need to break that number down into the different types of eye movement. How many of those eight times were moving forward, how many were moving back and how many were distracted glances to something else? This shows how much energy you spend fixating on words, a habit that speed reading will break you off. If the number of times you move your eyes is relatively low you won't have too much work to do. Additionally, if you rarely or never went backwards to reread text then you are doing pretty well already. However, you will probably discover that, like most people, your eyes move all over the place when you read. Needless to say, this significantly reduces your reading speed as well as your reading comprehension.

Do you vocalize words as you read them?

The chances are that as you are reading these words you are vocalizing them in your mind. This is a classic reading habit that is responsible for the average person having such a slow reading speed. Unfortunately, it is also one of the hardest habits to break. This is due to how the habit was formed in the first place. More often than not, the reason why a person vocalizes the words they read is that they were trained to do so. If you think back to when you learned how to read you will probably recall that your teacher had you read out loud at first. This was done so that your teacher could make sure you were pronouncing words correctly. After a while, when you proved that you could pronounce each and every word properly your teacher would tell you to stop reading out loud. They probably said something along the lines of "say it with your mind, not your mouth." And thus, the habit of vocalizing as you read was born.

Unfortunately, the age at which this instruction came along was one in which the average person is most impressionable. That is why this habit is so hard to break. Still, the important thing at this stage is to determine whether or not you commit this "reading crime." The main reason why this is such a problem is that it takes your mind longer to vocalize a word than it does to simply see a word. Therefore, as long as you "speak" the words in your mind you will never be able to improve your reading speed beyond a certain point, normally around 300 words per minute. Fortunately, there are several speed reading techniques that will help you to break this harmful habit.

Are you focused?

Finally, there is the question of how focused you are when you read. In order to determine this element choose something to read, set a timer for 5 minutes and read until the timer goes off. During this time count how many times you shift your attention from what you are reading to something else. Even if it is something else on the page, such as another line of text, a picture or a smudge mark, it counts. Needless to say, if you look up from your text that definitely counts! Simply count the number of times you are distracted in the 5 minute period. If this number is low then you already have good focus, therefore this isn't something you need to work on initially. However, if the number is high, such as 20 or more, then focus is something you will need to work on right away. The reason this is so important is that it takes your mind time to refocus on what you are reading each time you are distracted, which significantly lowers your reading speed. Fortunately, there are many speed reading tricks and techniques to help you fix this problem.

Chapter 3:
Breaking Bad Reading Habits

As with anything in life, the first thing you need to do in order to move forward with speed reading is eliminate the things that are holding you back. Bad habits are just as common in reading as they are in anything else. And, just as bad habits can keep a person from losing weight, getting a better job, or making any other significant improvement in their life, so too, they will keep you from successfully developing your speed reading skills. Therefore, before you start learning the different techniques that will greatly increase your reading speed and comprehension you must first identify and remove any bad reading habits you currently have. Don't be too disheartened if you suffer from most or all of the habits listed in this chapter. The truth is that these habits are very common to the vast majority of people, so you aren't alone! Fortunately, there are several simple yet effective methods for breaking these bad reading habits. This chapter will reveal those methods, thus enabling you to begin eliminating your bad reading habits right away.

Eliminate distractions

One of the main reasons why most people read at a slower speed is that they never pay full attention to what they are reading. The fact is that the brain can actually change its focus while you are reading, thereby causing the other senses to become heightened. As a result, your hearing, sense of smell and even sense of taste can begin to become more noticeable than normal, creating all sorts of distractions for your mind. The main reason for this is that when you read your eyes become focused on one thing instead of the countless things they normally see. This reduction in visual input causes your mind to look for input elsewhere. It's the same dynamic that occurs when you close your eyes. Therefore, it is critical that you take the necessary steps to eliminate any distractions that your other senses might pick up on.

Always make sure that you are reading in a relatively quiet place in order to avoid being distracted by different noises. One of the biggest mistakes most people make when reading is to read with a TV or radio on in the background. It is virtually impossible to focus on what you are reading when you have constant dialogue taking place for your ears to pick up on. Music can be a help or a hindrance depending on the person, so take the time to see if background music helps you to focus or if it distracts your attention. Other senses, such as your sense of taste and smell can be easily distracted if you are hungry. Therefore, always make sure you address such issues as being hungry or thirsty before settling down to read.

Another source of distraction can come from your mind itself. If you have an appointment later in the day you will become increasingly conscientious of the time, thereby creating a mental distraction that keeps you from fully focusing on what you are reading. Likewise, any to-do lists will tend to roll through your mind, constantly reminding you not to forget such things as going to the grocery store, answering an email, or any number of similar tasks. The best way to avoid such distractions is to take care of these tasks before you try to read any lengthy material. Only when your mind is clear of distractions will you be able to read at optimum efficiency.

How to stop word vocalization

As mentioned earlier, the act of vocalizing words as you read will significantly reduce your reading speed. This is because the average person can only speak at around 300 words per minute. Therefore, by vocalizing your words you create a fixed barrier that your reading speed will never be able to exceed. The good news is that even though this habit is both highly common and highly disruptive it can be broken. It will, however, take both time and effort to break completely. But it can be done.

The first method to breaking word vocalization is to create a distraction. This may seem counter intuitive since distractions can hinder your reading speed, however, a small distraction can stop the vocalization without having any negative side effects. One such distraction is to chew a piece of gum. The act of chewing will keep your mind from vocalizing words by tricking it. Simply put, when your mouth is chewing your mind will be less likely to vocalize anything since you might not be able to actually speak. In a way it's a bit like your mind practicing good manners. Since it's rude to talk while eating, your mind stops vocalizing while you are chewing. A piece of gum can keep you chewing for quite some time, thus enabling you to get a good bit of speed reading done without the inner dialogue.

Another distraction that can eliminate vocalizing the words you read is to listen to music while you read. Again, this will work better for some people as others might become too distracted by music. The important thing is to test different types of music in order to find one that does the trick. Something that most people find is that strictly instrumental music proves less distracting than music with vocals. This is because your mind tends to focus on any speech that it hears. Therefore, as instrumental music is free of speech it will be less distracting in a negative way. It will, however, create enough of a distraction to keep you from vocalizing written material.

If none of these methods helps to eliminate the inner dialogue you can always try counting while you read. This is the most complicated method, but it is one that tends to work when all else fails. The reason behind this is that you are breaking your habit of vocalizing the words you read by vocalizing something else, in this case counting. Once you develop the ability to read while counting in your mind you have effectively broken your habit of vocalizing what you read. The next step is to stop counting while you read, and then you're cured!

Learning to minimize eye movement while reading

Studies have shown that as the average person reads their eyes move in jerky motions in just about every direction. When moving forward your eyes will jump from the word you are reading to another word further down the line.

This random and erratic motion serves to significantly reduce anyone's reading speed. The simple truth of the matter is that you only read when your eyes are still. Therefore, the more your eyes move is the less you actually read. Thus, learning to minimize your eye movements is absolutely critical if you want to become a proficient speed reader.

The first method for learning to reduce your eye movement is to train your eyes to only move to certain points along any line of text. While you might think that you can only see one word at a time the fact is that your periphery vision allows you to see up to five or six words at once. Data collected from numerous studies suggests that you can see a couple of words to your left, and three to four to your right. This means that you can read an entire line of text by only focusing on a set number of spots along the line. If the line has twenty words you can read it with as few as three eye movements. Learning this process will increase your reading speed exponentially.

Perhaps the easiest and most effective method of training your eyes this way is to use an index card. Place the card over the line you are going to read and mark an 'x' over the first word. Place another 'x' four words further along. Repeat this for the length of the line. Once you have your card marked read the line by focusing your eyes only on the words below each 'x.' At first, this will be a bit strange, so you might not read all the words on the line. However, with a little practice you will develop your peripheral awareness, thus allowing you to see and take in the words your eyes aren't focused on. Eventually, you will be able to extend your markings, putting an 'x' over every fifth or sixth word. This process is known as "chunking," and it breaks you from the habit of focusing on each and every word of text. When you read "chunks" of words at a time it also helps to break you of vocalizing what you read, so it provides two benefits in one.

Breaking the habit of regression reading

The final habit that keeps most people from developing a good reading speed is that of regression reading. This is the act of skipping back to re-read text in order to better understand it. Needless to say, if you take one step back for every two steps forward it will take you that much longer to make any real progress. Unfortunately, most people have this habit, and it keeps them from achieving their true reading potential.

The good news is that this is probably the easiest habit to break. One simple method is to cover over the words you read as you read them. When the words are no longer visible you are less tempted to go back and look at them again. This process might slow your reading down a bit as you have to conscientiously keep up with covering the words you read, but it is an exercise that will be short lived. Once you break yourself of the temptation of re-reading text you can stop covering the words as you go. You don't have to cover more than the last few words to have the effect, so an index card will do just fine for the task.

Another way to avoid re-reading text is to use a pointer to "pull" you along the line of text. This is a method usually associated with increasing reading speed, but it can also serve to help keep you focused on the material ahead rather than the material behind. Again, you don't have to read with your finger moving along the lines of text forever, you only need to use this method until you break the habit of re-reading previous text. In the end you will discover that as you read forward any ambiguities or questions will be answered eventually, making regression reading completely unnecessary. More often than not pertinent information is repeated in any given text, therefore if you didn't get the information on the first time of reading you will get it again later on. Furthermore, context clues can help clarify questions throughout a written text, making it unnecessary to absorb each and every word along the way.

Chapter 4:
Creating Good Reading Habits

Now that you know the most common bad reading habits and how to overcome them it's time to start developing good reading habits. When you free yourself of the things holding you back and begin to practice positive habits and techniques you will unleash your true reading potential. Not only will you be able to read at a faster pace, but by practicing good reading habits you will increase your ability to disseminate and retain valuable information contained in any written text. Some of the most effective and commonly used good reading techniques may prove easier and less complex than you might expect. In fact, most good reading habits come down to nothing more than basic common sense. This chapter will reveal four of the best reading habits you can form to improve both your reading speed and comprehension.

Choose the right place and time

One of the biggest mistakes that most people make when it comes to reading is the time of day they choose to read in. Everyone knows that a person's physical energy levels fluctuate during the day, making certain times better for physical exertion than others. You wouldn't expect to find that mowing a lawn at midnight would prove as easy as if you performed the task during the early afternoon. Darkness aside, the fact is that you don't have the same energy at midnight as you do during the earlier hours of the day. Therefore, any task that requires physical exertion will prove more difficult as your energy levels decrease. The very same principle applies to mental exertion. Just as your physical energy is higher during the early hours of the morning, so is your mental energy higher as well. Thus, any mental activity will prove more difficult to perform late at night than it would have been during the earlier part of the day.

Subsequently, if you want to read with increased effectiveness and efficiency you need to choose a time when your mental energy is at its peak. While it's true that no two people are exactly alike, and thus, your energy levels may peak at different times, it's highly likely that your mind will be most attentive and capable during the late morning and early afternoon hours of the day. Even so, it's always best to discover your personal design in order to get the best results from your efforts. You can try reading at different times of the day to see which times work best for you.

Things you want to look for include how focused you are, how easily you can read the material, how quickly you can read the material and how much information you are able to retain. Once you find your best reading time it is important that you set that time aside for any lengthy or serious reading that you need to do.

Of equal importance to when you read is where you read. All too often people expect to be able to read anywhere just as they expect to be able to read at any time. Unfortunately, when you read in the wrong environment your attention can be seriously distracted, making reading an almost impossible task. Therefore, it is vital that you discover what environments work best for you when you need to do some serious reading. You might expect that the best place to read is somewhere quiet and isolated, however, this isn't necessarily true. While some people will find such environments ideal for reading others will find too much isolation or too much silence unsettling, creating considerable distraction as a result. Again, it is important that you take the time to discover what works for you. Read in several different places with different amounts of activity and noise. Once you discover the right environment for you make sure you do your reading in that environment whenever possible.

Choose the right material

Even though people's mental energy is higher earlier in the day than it is late at night, that isn't to suggest that you shouldn't read anything at night. Instead, it means that certain types of material should be avoided. Many people like to read before going to bed as it helps them to unwind and relax. However, if you choose this time to read an academic text or some sort of instructional material you will find your efforts all but wasted. The key is to choose the right material for different times of day. Any text that requires serious concentration and thought should be reserved for the times of day when your mind is at its strongest. Not only will this ensure that you read the material more quickly and easily, it also means that you will understand any valuable information it contains more readily.

Any night time reading should be restricted to fiction or light reading that requires less concentration than more academic texts. This type of writing is designed to activate the imagination more than the intellect, and thus it will be easier to read at the end of the day when your intellectual mind is tired and ready to rest. In fact, some people find it a struggle to read fiction during the day as their mind is more ready for an intellectual challenge than for engaging in fantasy and imagination. Still, these are generalizations, and the bottom line is that you need to find what works best for you. Try reading different types of texts at different times of day to determine which times prove best for each one. Then try to ensure that you read the right materials at the right times.

Learn to read content instead of words

If you read a book for the sake of relaxing and letting your mind drift off into the realm of fantasy then reading a text word for word is not necessarily a bad thing. However, if you are reading a text in order to acquire specific information then reading it word for word can, in fact, be a profound waste of time and energy. The simple truth is that there are two types of reading. First, there is reading for the sake of reading. This usually covers such genres as fiction, poetry and the like where each word can be instrumental at setting a scene or creating a mood. The second type of reading is reading for information. This is the type of reading you engage in when doing research, catching up on the news or reading instructional texts. It is also the type where reading word for word is totally unnecessary.

The trick to speed reading content for information is that you look for keywords. This allows you to see the content without having to pick through each and every word in the process. One way to ensure that you focus on content rather than words is to have a list of words that you are looking for. More often than not you will be looking to discover specific information within a given text. If you read the entire text you will wind up reading all sorts of information you didn't actually want or need. However, if you look for the information you need you can glance at a text and find it immediately. By focusing solely on the portions of text that contain the information you need you can reduce the amount of reading you do by up to seventy five percent. This is the act of reading content rather than words.

Exercise your mind

Finally, there is the factor that separates the true speed readers from all the rest. This is the habit of exercising your mind. Just as a person's body becomes stronger and capable of doing more as a result of physical exercise, so too, a person's mind reacts the same way to mental exercise. The more you exercise your mind is, the stronger and more capable it will become. Fortunately, it takes less time and effort to exercise the mind than it does to exercise the body. In fact, if you follow two specific exercises you will achieve any speed reading results you hope for with considerable speed and ease.

The first exercise is to increase your vocabulary. While a person's reading speed is usually reduced by such things as distraction, bad reading habits and the like the truth is that it can also be reduced by a small vocabulary. If you don't know a word, you will likely trip over it when you read it, as though it were a piece of furniture out of place. Therefore it is critical that you take the time and effort to increase your vocabulary knowledge in order to increase your reading efficiency. Fortunately, there are several ways in which you can achieve this goal. Daily calendars are available that have a different word each and every day, helping you to build your vocabulary in a relaxed but constant way. There are also online sources that offer a word a day or other such formats that introduce new words at a steady yet reasonable pace.

The second best exercise for your mind is simply reading more. As with every other thing in life, when it comes to reading practice makes perfect. People with the lowest reading speeds are often people who read the least amount of material. Alternatively, the more a person reads is, the better their reading speed and comprehension becomes. Therefore, perhaps the most critical element for developing the skill set of speed reading is your familiarity with reading itself. The more you read it, the more your mind will be comfortable with the process. Reading more will also help you to practice speed reading techniques more frequently, enabling you to master them even faster as a result.

Chapter 5:
Proven Speed Reading Techniques

The next step toward developing your speed reading skills is to begin practicing the most effective speed reading techniques. While there are several different techniques that can help to increase your reading speed and comprehension it only takes a few to make all the difference. In fact, it is recommended that instead of trying to learn all the techniques at once you should start with one or two, choosing to master those techniques before moving on to practicing the others. The following four methods are among the most proven speed reading techniques practiced by the pros. Once you begin practicing these methods you will notice results that are both immediate and highly significant. Needless to say, the more you practice these methods is, the better the results you will achieve. Some studies have shown that your reading speed will increase exponentially in as few as five weeks when you practice these methods each and every day.

Skim passages for pertinent information

One of the most widely used techniques within speed reading is what is called skimming. While the idea of skimming text may seem straightforward the fact is that it is often confused with its popular counterpart scanning. When you skim a text you read over the content looking for the important information contained within. Most of the time you won't necessarily know what this information is, meaning that you can't simply look for specific keywords. Instead you have to discover the information as you read along. This means that you will have to read a good percentage of the text, however, it does not mean that you have to read all of the text.

A simple method of scanning text is to read the first and last paragraphs of a section of text. This is easier to do when reading non-fiction as you can't necessarily skip entire stretches of fiction without losing important context and plot details. However, in the case of non-fiction material where information is usually addressed at the beginning of a section and reviewed at the end you can get all the details you need by reading these portions and skipping the middle altogether. The only thing you will miss by skipping middle portions is the exhaustive explanations of the topic being discussed. All pertinent information will be spelled out at the end, making that the most important piece of any non-fiction text.

The best way to skim a text is to come up with a list of questions in your mind regarding the information you are looking for. Such questions as *who, why, when* and *how* are the most useful when trying to get to the heart of a particular topic. If you can answer all of your questions after reading the beginning and end of a section then you know that you have obtained all the information you need, thus allowing you to move on. In addition to reading the beginning and end paragraphs you can also skim the headings of a section, descriptions below pictures, the table of contents and any other piece of text, which might contain condensed information. Sometimes you can get the gist of an article simply by reading its headings, subheadings and any bullet points contained within. This can save you from reading countless amounts of unnecessary text that only serves to increase the bulk of an article.

Scan text for keywords

Scanning is another proven technique for speed reading. While scanning may appear almost identical to skimming at first there is a very basic yet significant difference. When you skim a text you are looking for information that is unfamiliar to you. However, when you scan a text you are looking for information that you already know. One of the best examples of this is when you look for a particular movie or TV show in a list such as on Netflix or in the TV listings. When you are looking for something specific you pass over all of the information that doesn't match what you are looking for, making your search quick and efficient. Imagine how long it would take to find a movie or TV show if you actually took the time to read each and every word you came across. By the time you found what you were looking for it would have ended hours ago! Instead, you skip over non-essential text, searching instead for specific keywords, pictures or names. This is the art of scanning.

This practice is ordinarily used for locating specific information within a text for immediate use. Names, addresses, times and other detailed information are some of the more common examples of this type of information. Therefore, scanning isn't necessarily a technique you will use in regular reading, rather it is a technique that will only be used in specific circumstances. You can also scan a text to determine whether or not it contains enough pertinent information to actually read in greater depth. This is a highly effective technique for anyone doing research on a particular topic. Rather than reading countless articles you can narrow down your search by scanning each resource to determine its overall value. Not only will this save you time but it will also ensure that the reading you do is more productive.

Again, like with skimming you can focus on the beginning and end of a text, headings, tables, picture captions and the like. Since you are looking for specific keywords you will be able to scan any size text with a great deal of speed and ease. The more keywords that you find is, the more valuable a particular text will be. Alternatively, if you are unable to locate many or any keywords after a fair amount of scanning it is probably a safe bet that you should move on to another resource.

Change the order in which you read

Sometimes you might find that you have to read an entire text for one reason or another, meaning that scanning or skimming is out of the question. In such cases it might be tempting to simply revert to your old habit of reading a text word for word in the order it's written. Fortunately, there is a technique that can allow you to read a text completely yet with greater speed and understanding. This technique is changing the order in which you read. As mentioned earlier, most of the pertinent information in an article or informative text is contained in the beginning and end of the piece. Thus, if you read the beginning and end you will become familiar with the topic even if you previously had no knowledge of the topic at all. Once you have familiarized yourself with the material in this way you can read the middle portion with greater speed and ease. Since you will recognize the terms and concepts you can digest the more exhaustive text without any problems whatsoever. Therefore, if you have to read an entire text that is filled with detailed information, always read the beginning and end before reading the middle.

Another strategy is to read all of the information about the text that is available. Most books will have a brief description covering the content of the book, the author and any pertinent details about the topic being discussed. Most people skip such descriptions, viewing them as nothing more than promotional pieces designed to encourage a person to buy the book. However, skilled speed readers will recognize the value of these parts for the condensed information that they contain. In a way, reading any descriptive piece on a text is like watching the trailer of a movie. While the trailer doesn't provide the full content of the movie it gives you an idea of the characters, the plot and more often than not the outcome. When you go to see the movie after seeing its trailer you already have a sense of what to expect, allowing you to enjoy the subtle nuances of the movie that much more. This is the very same benefit you will gain when you read a description of a text before reading the text itself.

Read with purpose

In the end it comes down to one simple concept—reading with purpose. Whether you scan a text, skim a text or change the order in which you read a complete text, the key is to read for a specific reason. What slows most people down in their reading is that they read for the sake of reading, not for the sake of gathering information. However, when you read for the sole purpose of gathering information you will find that your reading habits change completely, allowing you to read in a fraction of the time while obtaining more information in the process.

Shopping is a great analogy for this. There are two basic types of shopping—window-shopping and hunting. When a person window-shops they tend to look at everything with little or no intention of actually buying what they see. They can spend all day window-shopping and not feel as though they have wasted any time. This is because they had no real agenda to start with. Instead, they simply wanted to spend their time wandering from one store to the next, seeing everything that is available. This is how most people read. They look at all of the words, taking everything in at an equal rate. Rather than looking for specific information they look at all the information, willing to take all the time in the world in the process.

Alternatively, there is the type of shopping known as hunting. This is when a person is on a mission to find and acquire a specific item. They may go to several stores in an attempt to find the best form of the item at the best price, but this is different from window-shopping. Even if the person goes to more than one store they won't spend much time in each, rather they will look to see if their item is available and if it's available for the right price. If it's not there, or if it's too expensive, they leave the store and move on to the next. Reading with purpose is like hunting. Instead of spending large amounts of time meandering through endless amounts of text you search for specific information. If a text contains that information you read it, but only as much as is necessary. If a text doesn't contain the information you leave it and move on. Just as a hunting-style shopping trip can take minutes as opposed to the hours spent window-shopping, so too, reading with purpose will reduce the time it takes to a readable text to a fraction of what it would take otherwise. Furthermore, you will always leave with exactly what you need—nothing more and nothing less.

Chapter 6:
Creating Your Daily Reading Practice

The importance of continuously practicing speed reading techniques cannot be overstated. Developing any skill requires constant work and dedication, and speed reading is certainly no exception to that rule. A good way to envision your speed reading development is to liken it to becoming a bodybuilder. One of the most effective ways of developing stronger muscles is to exercise on a regular basis. Equally important is to use the right exercises for your particular goals. Since some techniques for speed reading are designed for certain texts it is vital that you determine the type of reading you do in order to identify which speed reading techniques will be most beneficial for you. This chapter breaks down the different types of reading so that you can develop a daily routine that will help you to gain the best speed reading results possible. Whether you choose one or more of the techniques listed below, the most important thing is that you commit to practicing them on a daily basis. That is the only way to achieve the results you desire and deserve.

How to practice speed reading books

If you are the type of person who reads more fiction than anything else you will need to use the speed reading techniques that focus on reading an entire text more quickly and efficiently. One technique already mentioned is that of chunking words. This method requires a great deal of practice as it not only causes you to read faster, but it also causes you to read in a completely different way. The best way to practice this method is as follows:

- **Choose a simple text**. Just as a person who is new to lifting weights will start with lighter weights, so too, when you start practicing speed reading techniques you should begin with easier texts. The font size should be large enough to be able to read easily, and the words should be simple enough for you to understand. If you begin with a complicated text you will struggle with the text as well as the exercise, making your progress slower and more complicated than it has to be.

- **Start slow**. Chunking words is a method that you build over time. Rather than trying to read five or six words at once start by trying to just read two words at a time. This will help you to become familiar with the process without being overwhelmed by it. As you become accustomed to reading two words at a time you can increase it to three, then eventually four and even five.

- **Set a goal**. Another way to control the progress you make is to set solid goals for yourself. In the case of chunking words, you can set yourself the goal of becoming proficient at reading two words at a time in seven days. Take the next seven days to achieve the ability to read three words at a time. If you give yourself a week to develop each level you can progress at a steady yet significant pace. While a month may seem like a long time to complete this goal you have to realize that at the end of that month you will be reading four to five times faster than you do now. That's a pretty decent result to say the least!

- **Set aside quality time**. If you try to practice at different times of day, and in different environments, you will find your progress slower and less consistent. Therefore, it is critical that you set aside some quality time each and every day for your practice. By practicing at the same time and in the same conditions you can focus all of your energy on the exercise, thereby ensuring that you achieve the best results for your efforts.

How to practice speed reading news articles

Reading news articles is a different thing altogether from reading fictional texts. This means that the techniques needed for speed reading news articles will also be different. Skimming is probably the best method for getting pertinent information from any news oriented text, regardless of whether it's a newspaper, online article or some other similar format. The best way to practice skimming is as follows:

- **Create a list of questions**. As mentioned earlier, the best way to get information while skimming a text is to look for answers to specific questions. Therefore, the first thing you want to practice is the art of creating the questions. The best way to do this is to look at a news headline and ask what information you want to know about that particular topic. Once you have that list, read the entire article, without any concern over speed. Write down the pertinent information and compare it to your list. Did your questions cover everything or did you miss something? At first you might miss a question or two, however, when you practice this exercise a few times you will get the hang of knowing exactly what questions to ask in order to get all the important information.

- **Practice skimming**. Once you know what questions to ask you can begin to practice skimming in its entirety. Pick a news article, list your questions and skim for the answers. Focus on highlighted areas such as headlines, picture captions, quotes and any other text that stands out from the rest. See if you can't find all your answers in these key areas.

- **Build your speed**. Sometimes you will have to read entire portions of text in order to acquire the information you need. In this case you will want to practice reading lines of text quickly, usually using your finger as a guide to lead over the words in a quick and uniform way. The important element is gaining information, so only read as fast as you can while still being able to recognize important pieces of information as you come to them. As you develop this skill your speed will automatically increase, so you don't have to focus on it as much. Just remember, daily practice is the key to building your speed, so as long as you put in the effort you will get the results.

How to practice speed reading informational texts

Reading informational texts is similar to reading news articles, however, you will probably have some familiarity with the nature of the information you are looking for in this case. Subsequently, scanning is the method you will want to practice for this type of reading. As previously discussed, the key difference between skimming and scanning is that you will have a list of keywords to look for with scanning that you didn't have in the case of skimming. This makes all the difference between the two methods. The best way to practice scanning is as follows:

- **Identify primary targets**. The first thing you want to learn is what parts of a text are more likely to contain the information you are looking for. Take an article that you are already familiar with and come up with a list of keywords you know the article contains. Next, read the whole article, noting where each keyword is found. You can use a highlighter or simply circle the words as you find them. When you have read the whole article look at where the highlighted or circled words are. You will notice that they are clustered rather than spread out. Do this again on two or three other articles. In the end, you will notice a pattern as to where the keywords are most commonly located. These areas will be your primary targets.

- **Practice scanning unfamiliar articles.** Now that you have your primary targets identified you can see how effective they truly are by reading articles you are unfamiliar with. It is important that you have certain keywords to look for in these articles, however, as that is what is needed to perform the technique of scanning. When you have your keywords listed find as many as you can using only the primary targets. If you didn't find all of the words decide whether the missing ones are actually necessary, or whether the ones you found were enough. If the missing ones are necessary read the whole article in order to locate them. This will give you an idea of other targets to look for when scanning unfamiliar texts.

- **Build your speed.** Finally, practice scanning in a timed run. You can set a timer for one minute to start with, seeing if you can find all your keywords within that time. Once you can achieve that goal on a regular basis you can reduce the time by five seconds at a time. Eventually, you will be able to scan an article for as little as twenty seconds, obtaining all of the pertinent information you need within that time.

The need for discipline

It goes without saying that discipline is the key to achieving any level of success in any endeavor. Only when you put in constant effort and dedication can you hope to reach any goal. However, there can be many sides to discipline that are often overlooked. The key areas of discipline needed for developing your speed reading skills are as follows:

- **Practice daily**. You will have read these words several times already within this book, and you will probably read them several times more before the end. The main reason for that is because this is the most important element of developing your speed reading skills. If you stop practicing for any significant length of time you will begin to regress, meaning that your progress is not only slowed but actually reversed. Therefore, make sure that you practice each and every day so that your skills only ever get stronger.

- **Practice at a reasonable rate.** Sometimes you might be tempted to rush in and try to achieve results in less time by skipping steps or increasing the level of the challenge. While this won't be as dangerous as if you skipped ahead and began lifting heavier weights than you were ready for in the case of bodybuilding, it will still prove foolish. Developing any skill is a matter of progression. You need to learn to walk before you can run. Therefore, give yourself the right amount of time to ensure that you develop your skills properly.

- **Repeat steps when necessary.** Certain skills will require more time than others. This is simply due to the fact that different people have different inherent abilities that enable them to excel at certain things. However, there will be some things you don't excel at. If you need to repeat a step or add time on to a particular practice, then do so. Never push on for the sake of pushing on. Always make sure that you have fully developed each skill before starting on the next. It takes considerable discipline to know when you aren't ready to move on.

Chapter 7:
Some Simple Exercises

There may be times when you aren't able to read much on a particular day. It stands to reason that your schedule might change unexpectedly from time to time, disrupting your day-to-day routine. Fortunately, this isn't necessarily a problem. In the event that you can't devote the time and energy to reading your regular amount of material you can choose to perform quick and easy exercises to help keep your speed reading skills sharp. The following are some examples of these exercises, along with some additional online tools that will help improve your speed reading development.

Practice reading with a timer

This is an easy exercise that can be performed with any of the speed reading techniques covered. You can choose to read a portion of text within a given amount of time to ensure your reading rate is at its peak, or you can test yourself on such techniques as skimming or scanning to determine your rate at acquiring specific information. The important thing is to develop a timed exercise that suits your needs. In the event that you read regular text you can set a timer for two minutes and count the number of words you have read within that time. Even though this may not seem like much it will help to keep your mind ready and focused for when you do return to reading lengthier passages.

When it comes to practicing timed runs with skimming and scanning the focus is on information rather than word count. Set a timer for sixty seconds and skim or scan your chosen document. When the timer goes off see if you have acquired all of the necessary information. Needless to say, the time you set will decrease as your skills improve, thus the sixty second time is just an example. You may want to set the time for thirty seconds to give you an extra challenge. If you have a timer app on your phone or a timer on your watch you can perform this exercise anytime, anywhere. You can even practice while in a waiting room, online at the supermarket, or even waiting for a train. All you need is access to an informative document, a timer and a moment to yourself.

Highly effective eye exercises

One thing that can help to increase your speed reading results is to regularly exercise your eyes. This makes perfect sense since it's your eyes that are doing all of the physical work. If your eyes are weak your reading speed will suffer as a result. Therefore, increasing the health and strength of your eyes is a vital process with regard to improving your speed reading skills. The following are a few examples of eye exercises that you can do anytime and anywhere:

- **Eye squeezes**. This exercise should actually be called "face squeezes" as it addresses the muscles in your face and neck as well. You can do this exercise any time you have three or so minutes of uninterrupted time to spare. First, slowly take in a deep breath, opening your mouth and eyes as wide as possible in order to stretch your facial muscles. Next, exhale slowly, closing your eyes as tightly as you can while also squeezing the muscles of your head, neck, face and jaw. Maintain this position while holding your breath for about 30 seconds. Repeat the process three or four more times for best results.

- **Eye writing**. This exercise strengthens your eyes by making them move in ways they are unaccustomed to. Most of the time your eyes move up and down or side to side. However, this exercise will increase the range of your eye motion by making your eyes move in various directions. First, focus on a wall that is fairly far away from you. Next, pretend that you are using your eyes to write your name on the wall. In other words, move your eyes along the same way you would a pen when writing your name. The different motions will increase the strength and dexterity of your eyes.

- **Thumb-to-thumb glancing.** This exercise is similar to eye writing, although it focuses solely on the side-to-side motion of your eyes. Start by looking straight ahead, extending your arms to your sides. Stick your thumbs straight up, as though you are hitching a ride. Next, look back and forth between your left thumb and your right thumb ten times without moving your head. Rest your eyes for 30 seconds and repeat three more times.

Test your comprehension

As mentioned earlier, speed reading is as much about comprehension as it is about speed. Being able to read 600 words per minute is of no value if you don't understand or retain what you read. Therefore, you will want to test your comprehension as often as you test your reading speed. This is a fairly simple process, requiring nothing more than answering a few questions after you read a portion of text. In fact, you can incorporate this test with the timed reading tests. After you complete a timed run on reading, skimming or scanning take a moment to ask yourself the nature of what you just read. If you are reading a work of fiction try to recall the events you read in as much detail as possible. List off the characters involved, the locations, and any events that took place. The more detailed your recollection is, the better since this shows that you have a high comprehension rate.

When you test your skimming and scanning using a timed run you will automatically test your comprehension when you try to list the information you obtained at the end of the exercise. In the case of skimming you should be able to answer the basic questions of who, why, where, what and how. If you cannot answer any of these questions you can either increase the time you set for your runs, or you can keep practicing with the shorter time. When you can answer all of the questions within the time allotted you can reduce the time, thereby developing your skills even further.

Additional tools for improving your skills

There are an increasing number of online apps that will help you to hone your speed reading skills. Each app offers a different range of tools and text availability, so it is important that you take the time to research each app in order to know the one that is best suited to your needs. Furthermore, not all apps are compatible with all devices, so be sure to check compatibility before making your purchase. Here are four of the more popular speed reading apps available:

- **ReadMe**. ReadMe is an e-reader app that can be integrated with other speed reading tools to help you to increase your reading speed quickly and easily. You can store your personal library onto ReadMe, which will enable you to speed read familiar material. When used with BeeLine Reader your material will have color added to the words, effectively guiding your eyes along the lines of text in a natural and effective way. This will increase your reading speed while training your eyes to avoid regression reading. When used with Spritz you can read your favorite books one word at a time, with each word being flashed onto the screen so that you can reduce your eye movement to an absolute minimum. It is compatible with both iPhone and Android devices.

- **Accelerator**. Unlike ReadMe, Accelerator does not act as a personal library. The main function of this app is to enable you to speed read news articles, text documents from your personal email account or certain online news and article apps. This app is reminiscent of the reading tests many people get in grade school where a document scrolls along at a set pace, determining your reading speed. The pace is adjustable, so you can use this app to increase and monitor your reading rate. This app is only compatible with iPhone or iPad.

- **Outread**. This app is perhaps one of the most versatile of all speed reading apps. You can choose to download any eBook you own to the app, upload a Word document, pick a book from the app's extensive library, or read text from online pages by pasting URLs or linking to specific newsreader apps. Outread will present the text by either flashing one word at a time or by highlighting a word at a time from a fully visible text. Additionally, a daytime and nighttime mode allows you to adjust the brightness of your screen to make reading more comfortable on your eyes. This app is compatible with iPhone or iPad devices.

- **Spreeder**. Perhaps one of the most comprehensive speed reading apps, Spreeder provides not only the tools needed for practicing speed reading, but it also provides access to reports that show your progress as well as guided training regimens. You can upload files to read, access books from your cloud library, or directly link to websites to create an unlimited selection of reading material. The basic app is free to use, but you can purchase an upgrade that will take your speed reading training to a whole new level. Spreeder is compatible with a whole range of devices, including iPhone, iPad, Mac, Web and Windows.

Conclusion

Now that you have read this book you have all the tools you need to develop your speed reading skills. By identifying and breaking your bad reading habits you can free yourself from all of the behaviors that have served to slow you down. Once your bad habits are gone you can replace them with those that will help you to increase your reading speed by three to four times. Finally, you can choose the speed reading techniques that are right for the style of reading that you do on a regular basis. Whether you read for pleasure, for work or just to stay caught up on current events, you can do so in a fraction of the time while gaining more information than ever before. The important thing is to practice every day, even if it's just for a few minutes. By practicing regularly you will develop your ability to read faster than ever, even getting to the place where you can read as much as a book a day!

www.ingramcontent.com/pod-product-compliance
Lightning Source LLC
LaVergne TN
LVHW012017060526
838201LV00061B/4343